MenSpeak

An Intimate Look at the Male Experience and Spirit

Paul Mott

Published in Australia by
Four Cs Media
Fitzroy 3065 Australia
+61400 466 998
Email: paulmottauthor@gmail.com
Websites: www.paulmottauthor.com
www.menspeak.co

First published in Australia 2015

National Library of Australia Cataloguing-in-Publication data

Creator: Mott, Paul, author.
Title: MenSpeak : an intimate look at the male experience and spirit / Paul Mott.
ISBN: 9780994181602 (paperback)
Subjects: Men--Psychology.
Men--Conduct of life.
Masculinity--Social aspects.
Dewey Number: 155.332

Cover design by PixBeeDesign and FayeFaye Designs
Set in 11.7/16.2pt Adobe Caslon Pro by David Schembri Studios

This book is dedicated to the men that I sat with over many years who were willing to share who they are and what they experience and were willing to connect with other men in ways that transcended their everyday experience.

Praise for *MenSpeak*

The book encapsulates the hidden and mysterious radiance of the male soul, expressed under very special conditions.

For a younger man, this book could be an epiphany, the wisdom of twenty-four fathers!

I am now sixty-nine. With these words have come wonderful memories, of the men who spoke them and the places I heard them spoken.

MenSpeak is a product of this energy, the power of good men.

Dr John Buckingham, Dentist

MenSpeak took me deep into the male psyche; a place one rarely gets the opportunity to go, especially a female. Taboo it's been.

Everyday life just simply doesn't give us ***MenSpeak***. The book does.

MenSpeak helped me much better understand, be aware of, and come to terms with the skin-deep and complex dynamics of the male and female exchange.

Veneta Tsindos, Journalist and Author

MenSpeak juxtaposes the sad, silly stuff that most of us men do for most of our lives with examples of ways to have a different experience. It seems that many of us are trying to be good, strong men, but find ourselves only knowing how to be angry or withdrawn when things get complex.

So men: what are we waiting for? Surely it is time to be courageous enough to set aside patterns of behaviour that do not seem to be helping, to explore the road less travelled, and to give ourselves the chance of arriving somewhere new.

Dr. Peter Howe, Staff Specialist Anaesthetist at the Royal Children's Hospital, Melbourne, Australia.

Reading ***MenSpeak*** has reminded me again how hard it is for men. I have used it several times to open a conversation with my husband: 'Is this true for you?' or 'This sounds like us sometimes'.

I long again to sit in a circle, with men and women speaking truly and honestly being themselves.

Deborah Vaughan, Artistic Director

Dear reader, if you are a man, my wish for you is ***MenSpeak*** touches your heart and you recognize yourself in the words of the men. May you find your own way back to your Self.

If you are the partner of a man and you sense that he is somewhere behind the wall, my wish for you is that this book opens your understanding and your heart. May you stand with courage, patience and love beside the man who needs to find his own way to his Self.

Graeme Vaughan, Strategic Planning, Department of Health and Human Services, Hobart, Australia

MenSpeak delves into the psyche and spirit of men – historically, in the present, and how this understanding can affect the future of male generations to come.

MenSpeak gave me greater insight into my husband and son, and our family dynamic. It invites introspection, and that's the best place to start the journey of self-understanding, healing and life-betterment.

Amanda J Spedding, Author and Editor

Contents

Asian and Chinese philosophy use a circle divided by an S-shaped line into a dark and light segment, describing how seemingly polar opposites or contrary forces are interconnected and interdependent in the natural world, representing respectively yin and yang combination or fusion of the two cosmic forces, each containing a 'seed' of the other. I have always loved the book of I-Ching where the two Chinese characters for I (meaning easy or change) and Ching (meaning profound book) represent the sun (Yang) which is usually on top and moon (Yin) on the bottom. I chose this symbol and put the dark side on the top to represent that men are often seen to present their dark side in their personal and professional lives, and yet, under the right conditions so easily reveal their light side.

MenSpeak

The male spirit hurts. It has been hurt. And for too long it has returned or transferred that hurt to others physically, verbally, emotionally, psychologically, spiritually and to itself.

This book is about expressing that hurt and then healing through empathic listening with deep, soft curiosity to other men speaking. You will experience men willing to reopen wounds and allow you to enter into what the male spirit experiences. Then, to go through the wounding experiences to the lightness of being a lovable, loving and aware connected Self.

This book is intended for all men. It is also for everyone whose male spirit longs to be expressed without harshness, criticism, sarcasm, hurt, ridicule and blame, accusation, non-acceptance, disapproval and fear.

Introduction

In 1988 I began facilitating a men's group at the request of several men I was working with at the time. They encouraged me saying there were no support groups for men to share their experiences and express their feelings in a safe environment. The group started with about 15 men and we met at my house, and then at various other venues over the 15 years of its existence.

The purpose of *The Men's Group* (which simply became its name) was to have a gathering of males, in a supportive environment, learn to explore and bring to life their own inner realities. What was evident over time, and what so often came through their speaking, was that women raised the men, often with little or no input from other males. Although this is slowly changing, this appeared to adversely affect their relationships with women, other males and, particularly, themselves.

The Men's Group addressed these issues as well as other issues such as anger, rage, aggressiveness, emotional dependence, sadness, grief, feelings of powerlessness and not being able to express a range or depth of feelings. Also so often experienced, regardless of the level of the men's external level of 'success', was rejection and a sense of not being good enough. The group was experiential, utilizing body, movement, mind and meditative, relaxing and spiritual processes, psychodrama, family of origin dynamics, open forum discussions, dream work and individual and group rituals and rites of passage.

As a result of the group process, participants found they gained insights and support when difficult situations and experiences arose. With each session, participants also found they had a greater sense of self-acceptance and peace towards themselves and others.

A connection (not previously experienced) with other men had a powerful, positive impact on the men's lives. The collective energy of the group also enabled participants to reshape their father/son/brother experience. *The Men's Group* also seemed to affirm men's experience of being male.

The group went through many stages. Men could come and go. There was no obligation to stay for any length of time, and yet, there were about a dozen men who stayed with the group from its inception. After eight years of meeting, so many topics and experiences had been covered. Again, with the urging of some of the participants, I set out to address, in written form some of the experiences that had been recurring and moving themes. I asked 24 of the men to come together, and through several processes that introduced various recurring themes, to write on nine of the topics most raised over the years.

The nine topics chosen, of which most of the men wrote, were:

1 **Relationships and the Rationing of Love:** What men find the hardest in relationships and what causes them to hold back.

2 **Intimacy and Commitment:** Words that sometimes strike terror in men; what they want but don't know how to achieve.

3 **Criticism, Blame, Sarcasm and Accusation:** When expressed by a partner, experienced as so crippling to their spirit, energy, creativity and well-being.

4 **The Spiritual Man:** What spirit is to the men and how they expressed it.

5 **Cycles, Seasons and Tides:** What metaphorical cycle, season and/or tide each man felt he was in and what that felt like.

6 **My Eulogy:** Each man summing up his life.

7 **Looking Back:** Projecting themselves forward into the middle of the 21st century, the men looked back to the times already experienced in the lives and wrote what life was like for them.

8 **Fathers:** Each man was asked to express what his experience of his father was like for him.

9 **The Movement of Men:** Finally, each man wrote of his experience in being involved in a men's group, with a view to encouraging other men to make an inward journey.

The subject matter of this book had been addressed in many forms over the years that *The Men's Group* met. I wanted what each man wrote about to be reflective of the content and give a sense of the issues and processes that men experienced over the years in *The Men's Group*.

The book is a compilation of men speaking on topics that recurred over the years the group met. My main difficulty in putting this book together was to keep my views to an absolute minimum. My original idea was to simply produce just what the 24 men wrote on the topics, without comment.

I was increasingly convinced to say more as the facilitator and compiler of the work, which has led to the following structure:

Part I is my commentary on what the men have said, interspersed with quotations from the transcripts. Some readers may prefer to start here, and refer to the transcripts later. My reader group was somewhat divided as to whether the transcripts should come first or my commentary. Either way is fine.

Part II consists of the transcripts in their entirety, unedited except for minor corrections of syntax to make them easier to read. The reader may wish to begin here.

I hope that this book encourages men to begin or continue a journey of self-discovery as one of the most inspiring aspects to their life.

I invite you to sit with this book and to ponder the wonderment of the male experience and spirit... without criticism, without sarcasm, without rejection, without fear.

For years I have invited groups to listen to others as if they are listening to aspects of themselves being given a voice (on their behalf) and finally speaking to them. I now invite you to read and then internally listen to aspects of yourself speaking to you through each man's experience. I invite you to read non-judgmentally, allowing the experience in. After sitting with it for a while, what does not fit for you will dissipate, leaving just what is right for you. I invite you to enter a world of which you have always known but may not have known how to access – the world of the male experience, the male spirit.

One final note for any health-care professional who may be reading this book: I invite you to resist the temptation to analyse and intellectualize what you read through your existing diagnostic filters and instead allow yourself to just sit with what men speak when they feel the freedom to speak.

Thank you,

Paul Mott

PART I

MenSpeak

Chapter 1

Why the book, *MenSpeak?*

This book is for men and women, being spoken to by men. It is for men and women who want to read what men speak when they are given the safe environment and the invitation to speak from an extraordinary place within themselves.

This book is not to address complicated or complex psychological, cultural or political issues related to men. The book is intended for men who would (or may) not otherwise enquire into themselves because the information presented is too distant from their own experience to be able to relate to it.

This book is intended to encourage men to begin a journey of greater self-discovery and expression.

I hope that men will be inspired to be curious and begin a journey of self-discovery as a result of what is presented in this book and the men who have spoken. I also hope that if you are reading this book it is because you are interested in what men have to say so that you can better understand, have empathy for and share in the experience of what men share with each other.

This book will benefit men who seek to know themselves better and be in more loving relationships with themselves, their families, their partners and their communities. It will benefit partners of men who are seeking a more insightful, intimate and expressive relationship with the men in their lives. I often hear men say that for women to understand men, women need to have empathy and understanding for the younger parts of men that have been hurt, and, to some degree, will always be vulnerable.

This book is also written because of how difficult it sometimes seems for men and women to get along and enjoy being with each other. So many people I have seen over some 30 years in private practice are in pain. Men are trying to be better partners and women are asking, 'Why can't men be intimate, committed, trusted and willing and able to express their feelings?'

It is important for men to know, understand, gain insight into and change themselves if they want to be in more openly expressive and loving relationships. I have found the following influences enable men to make the transition from closure to openness.

- ***The inner self:*** *men knowing their 'inner Self' and learning how to spend more of their time somewhere different to their various facades.*

- ***Family of origin:*** *realizing the influence of the family of origin and the wounds men may have received.*

- ***Protections and defenses:*** *gaining insight into the protections and defenses that men have needed to construct to protect and defend their wounds and vulnerabilities at various stages of their lives to keep them safe.*

- ***Stages of life:*** *men experiencing how pain and wounds can occur in different ways at various stages of life.*

- ***The vulnerable middle years:*** *understanding what can be accomplished in the crisis state, especially gaining insight into the various crises during the middle years.*

- ***Men in relationships:*** *understanding relationship dynamics.*

- ***Rationing Love:*** *learning to move into the fullness and abundance of love.*
- ***Choice:*** *learning how to move from anxiety and reaction to creating proactive ways of being.*
- ***The spiritual man:*** *the unfolding of the inner man leading to men making decisions on how they are in the world.*

A crime against men is that they have been taught to conceal their feelings. So many men have been shamed in their families by their fathers (when relating to their mothers) and their mothers (when being too much like their fathers), as well as on the streets, schools, playgrounds and public arenas where sensitivity was not accepted and usually ridiculed. One man in *The Men's Group* said *'I always hoped that there might be a place where speaking would be so different. On the first day it took such courage just to walk from the car to the door. And what a difference it has made.'*

Normally, in being with men, speaking tends to be an assessment of life. Men often seem to assess their lives rather than share their experiences. In this book you will see how quickly men can move from speaking from the heart to a safer teaching, conceptualizing, philosophizing posture. Sometimes, there is a *talking about* their experience but not necessarily an *expression of* their experience.

In *The Men's Group*, the room would go silent, and it was like a different energy came into the room, a different feeling when a man started speaking from the heart. And they all expressed how they felt vulnerable, and it is often that vulnerability that stopped them from sharing. It stops them because they wondered how they could function, do their work *and* feel vulnerable. How could they negotiate in meetings, be strong, be with males in the male world, hold their power... if they allowed vulnerability?

In the group, often we would hear regression occurring and the men seemed to feel how they felt when they were children. The main purpose of the group was for men to learn ways to *process* this, understand themselves and make the changes in their lives that brought a sense of wholeness and self-acceptance.

Usually it was the pain in the non-relationship the men were having with a partner that brought them to seek counseling either privately or as part of *The Men's Group*. Men tended to attend, most often, in their late 20s, 30s, and 40s usually feeling stuck behind the façade in preparation for the next decade.

Chapter 2

Knowing the 'Self'

I have mentioned terms such as the loss of Self or one's inner world. I have presented that when we lose the ability to access that inner Self it is very difficult to be in an intimate relationship. Intimacy requires the expression of our feelings and appropriately and successfully expressing our needs.

But what is the Self that I am talking about? It can easily be seen as who it is that we are having the conversation with… a voice (or voices) always going on within us. It can also be viewed as a combination of feelings, emotions and thoughts, or even body sensations. The Self is not necessarily a static or set presence; it is constantly changing.

The inner Self was also referred to as soul or spirit. Sometimes it was expressed as the sense of who we *are,* which is not necessarily connected to (or an expression of) what we *do, have* or *accomplish.* One man said he thought of the Self as what is not there when we die.

Men elaborated on this, suggesting the Self is what exists outside the body at the time of death. They chose words like 'life force, spirit, soul, energy and essence' of what is no longer in the body. If who we *are* is based on *doing* and *having,* we are incredibly vulnerable to losing what we do or have or may therefore feel we have, come to an end.

The outer adapted self

The outer adapted self is an external self we present to the world, each year adding more adaptive layers. It is mostly in the mind (particularly the left brain that is rational, logical and is a keeper of 'the facts'). From this aspect, men learn to do, to fix, to analyze, and to operate.

The inner Self

The inner Self is more than our mind. It includes our bodies (how we feel physically, inside) and our feelings, both of which require our attention, so that we can get to 'know' ourselves. The internal Self is that part of a man that feels, dreams and allows him 'to be'. It is in this state 'of being' that he can journey into an even deeper inner Self.

It is very powerful when a man has a balance of both the internal and external self. The beauty about being able to access the inner Self is that a man has the ability to know his *body, mind* and *feelings* and is better able to *process*, which is a deeper, richer experience than just analyzing. Learning to *process* is important because it incorporates both the *masculine* and *feminine*. It is a body, mind and feeling experience.

Before continuing, let me briefly state, for the context of this book, what is meant by the *body, mind* and *feelings*, and define *processing*, the *masculine* and the *feminine*.

Body, mind, feelings

If we do not know ourselves at the physical and emotional level, our understanding of what is happening with us will only be at the analytical (*mind*) level. This analytical (*mind*) level of viewing the world is good to a point because it enables us to make decisions. However, decisions based only on analysis are limited, as are decisions that are based only on our feelings would also be limited.

Our *body* and *feelings* also gives us warning signals of what is happening to us so that we can make adjustments. For example, we may (physically) feel a tightening in our stomach, which can tell us that we are feeling fear. This (emotional) feeling of fear is something we need to listen to and be curious about so that we do not push or protect our *bodies* or *feelings* excessively. Our *bodies* and *feelings* need to be experienced *and* expressed. Our *body* and *feelings* allow us to experience the world more fully. Our *mind* helps us make sense of the world around us and is also available to help us make sense of the world (our *body* and *feelings*) we are in and that is within us.

Processing

What I mean by *processing* is utilizing our body, mind, feelings and our understanding of our past patterns in gaining insight into the fullness of what is happening in our lives. If we do not learn this we tend to relate to life with a simple 'cause and effect' reasoning. This is efficient, but impractical, particularly in relationships.

For example, a man might decide that a particular event caused a particular outcome, as if there was no choice in the matter. It is viewed as 'This happened, so this was the effect'. By *processing* the event, he may discover that he can intervene and change the way that circumstances unfold by changing the way he experiences the event, rather than by trying to change the event itself. For many, this results in men owning what they experience rather than the powerless position of blaming others.

Men with little access to the Self who, for example, have extramarital affairs have often said things like, 'It just happened to me'; or men have related engaging in anger-fuelled violence as if something outside themselves was the cause of their actions.

In *processing*, a man realizes he can intervene and change the effect of an event by how he views and experiences the event, rather than feeling at the effect of the event. So many people in counseling sessions say how they get so frustrated when things do not work out the way they want. When they learn how to *process,* their emphasis moves from changing the world to changing themselves in getting what they want from the world around them.

Masculine and feminine

Somewhat following on from this, when decisions are based on a state of 'wholeness', a man has respected what we might call his masculine and feminine energy.

Masculine energy describes the logical, reasonable, action-driven, doing, task-oriented, event-oriented, analytical, problem-solving approaches in our interaction with people, events and the world around us. Feminine energy involves being open, receiving and curious. Men (and women) are a combination of both masculine and feminine energy.

Men (and women) can be out of balance when they accept too much of either masculine or feminine energy. Or, like with a picture the masculine or feminine energy can be either not developed or not fully developed. It often comes out (is developed) in dreams.

I want to be clear in this conversation that this section is not about sexuality or sexual preference. This is about energies that seem to 'take us over' at times in our lives. Both men and women can be overly masculine or feminine. A man can be in too much feminine energy; likewise, a woman can be in too much masculine energy.

Masculine and feminine energy and couples

Now, imagine the dilemma of many professional couples today that both operate in masculine energy while at work. They both come home requiring softness, nurturing and caring – or as one man said, "To someone who is keeping the home fires burning." This is a wonderful metaphor both for the feminine and 'the mother'. Such a couple is expressing a need or yearning for some feminine, nurturing energy to come home to. No one is there to give it. The couple experiences each other from a state of depletion, hoping to get something yet so little is available.

Issues related to losing the Self

Loss of the Self is when a man is not aware or consciously experiencing that the Self exists, that there is someone to whom the conversation within us is being directed.

For example, there is the issue of men not knowing when they are being abused or wounded. Take Xavier, who came to see me at the age of 42. Xavier had been protecting himself for so long that he actually could not tell when he was being hurt. His partner was very critical. When asked if it was all right for him to be in a relationship with a woman who criticizes continuously, Xavier said, "I don't know. In my mind I'd like to hear other things. But at a feeling level I do not know if it is wounding me or not." (However, he is prone to sporadic rages where he feels he could absolutely go crazy.)

Another way of losing your Self is not knowing how to nurture your Self, giving your Self that tenderness, soothing and warmth that comes from the feminine aspect of us. Without knowing our own feminine nurturing side we could search for years for the right woman to give us what we want, but do not feel we can give to our Self.

Nurturing the Self

The difficulty in nurturing the Self usually comes from looking for either a strong masculine (to look after, protect or defend us) or a strong feminine (to care for, nurture, be open and expressive to us) energy in someone else. What happened with Xavier, who had a beautiful wife and two daughters, is that the wife was more wedded to her country and family of origin and her daughters than she was to Xavier. Xavier worked long hours, provided well for his family but experienced his life as an interloper in his own family. The harder Xavier worked to provide for his family (he stated 'to mainly fulfill his wife's needs') the less he received and the more he was criticized for not being at home and being there for his wife and daughters.

Men want to be nurtured but often have learnt to go into 'nurturing energy' by looking after, providing for and protecting/defending another, rather than just being there as a listener, lover and receiver, open to just hearing what a woman has to say. Not feeling as though he has to do something about what she says. Just receiving. Many men are surprised to learn that the person they are trying to nurture would prefer them to simply listen and receive, without feeling that they have to do something about what they are hearing. This listening is accomplished through being soft, warm and curious.

Chapter 3

Family of Origin and Fathers

Our family of origin experiences are immeasurably strong influences on how we see our role, the rules we live by, our values and beliefs, how we view life, what we like and dislike and how we interact with ourselves, others and the world.

What men have learned from their childhood experiences greatly influences how they are experiencing the world today. For example, if a young boy witnessed domination and control, I find that they tend to go any of three ways: they are compliant and try to please and be *really, really* good; or they avoid relationships (or will only go so far into a relationship before getting out); or they are dominating and controlling.

If the father is absent (physically, psychologically, emotionally and/or even creatively and many men seem to have had this experience) then, again, they act *really, really* good, in an attempt to get the father back. Or they may act out in other ways, such as avoiding relationships, pretending their early experiences didn't really hurt them; or dominating and controlling, particularly acting out aggressively. Many of the men in the group over the years spoke lovingly of their mothers but also acknowledged their mothers often overcompensated for their father's absence.

Adam

I learned that to follow your moral value base meant that you would be comfortable with your decisions but not always with the outcomes. I learned that family and community were important and that we should contribute of ourselves. I learned that we have choices in how we are in a situation. I wish he had taught me that I should focus more on myself, that I was as important as family and community.

That to subjugate my SELF for others all the time would lead to a draining of SELF. I wish he would have spent more time with me just letting me be, instead of always telling how I could or should improve or do better. I wish he had told me I was OK more often. I wish he had more of himself to give to me when he was around rather than spending himself on other kids or things so that when there was time for me he was tired or angry or critical or punishing me. I wish we could have been light and played, as I grew older, not just when I was a young child. I wish he hadn't shown how the faults/downfalls of others could disappoint so much. I wish he could have worked less and been lighter.

Brett

Did learn not to judge others, stoically grin and bear it, hard work (physical and mental) pays off, constancy, the subtlety of conveying affection, to be tough, to be cynical, to beware, to be stable. I learnt from my father that life can be cruel and hard and that talk is cheap. I learnt that compromise should not be entered into easily and that privacy (a man's home is his castle) is the peak experience. I would have liked to learn more about kindness in the family, about warmth and caring. I would also have liked to learn more about how to deal with pent-up anger effectively. Family pride he taught me but it wasn't always something to be proud of. Perseverance (of an ill) is not always a good thing.

Did not have him take me to my footy matches as a junior. When he did turn up it was like he was being critical. I did not learn how to take criticism well from my father. I doubt that I handle criticism of my son all that well. I would have liked praise when it was due.

Carl

I learnt how not to do it; that is by living the experience of my relationship with my father. I have been able to have the relationship with my sons that I did not have with my father. There have been lessons that I did not learn at times. I repeated the cycle sometimes and this seemed to be more with my eldest son when he became a teenager. I suppose I was always a positive sort of person. My father was extremely negative and I have seen the damage that he has caused amongst my brothers and sisters. My eldest son tends to be negative at times and I find that difficult to cope with because it is my father and I all over but in reverse roles.

Sometimes I lack a lot of confidence and whilst on the surface I appear to others as being in total control, I am actually proving to my father that I am good enough but always fearful of failure. Through the men's group I was able to learn how to address a lot of these issues with my father before he died. I wished he had been more open and intimate with me. And I wish he had been more reassuring rather than the constant negatives which actually spurred me on.

I wished that he would actually touch or hug me. He finally did when he was over 70 years of age. I am not missing that opportunity with my own sons.

Darren

I am so scared that you'll die. I wish you'd have been around more to play with me, to help me, to kick a footy more than the two times I can remember, to play cricket more than the once or twice. To teach me how to hold a cricket bat, even though you didn't know.

You did know camping. Why didn't we go camping more? Why did you leave Mum in front of the TV so often so many years? You withdrew. If you die soon, you'll leave our family with a feeling of repressed emotion. I wish I knew you well enough to be angry with you sometimes. I got from you an enormous capacity to love at a community and platonic level but a difficulty expressing it on a person-to-person level – we needed a special occasion to feel it. Such moments were great, but love was very rarely expressed for the hell of it.

I got your hands and feet. I love them. I got your love of nature, plants, country, and the wild. I got your deep sadness when your Mum died, when you took that phone call in the front hall when I was about seven. How hard was it, knowing that we hated her?

I got your sense of being busy doing things that can't be criticized. I got your love, but your strangled inability to show it easily. I got your wisdom. I hope you don't die for a long time.

If the mother is *really* (overly) involved with the son (particularly in the absence of the father), then the son tends to grow up comparing women with his mother. Men do this by either continuing to *really, really* please women and then feeling disappointed when '*the women are not perfect*'. Or, they avoid relationships by only allowing women to have 'so much' of them, (kind of rationing themselves as a defense mechanism). Or men can attempt to dominate women to change them (so they are more like their mother). Men are usually unaware of this of course, and possibly even deny that this dynamic is really even being played out.

No matter what the background, parents who have not worked through their own childhood pain have brought up children. So many men who find themselves in therapy have experienced a dominating power play between the parents in so many expressions, such as:

Dominant Mother with **Passive, Not Present Father**

Dominant Father with **Passive, Compliant Mother**

When brought up in such a setting, the child can find it difficult to hold onto his 'real' self. He is too vulnerable.

And the power struggle between the parents is not necessarily demonstrated verbally. Men have expressed that sometimes it was just an *'energy'* between the parents that seemed to rob their younger selves from feeling safe, cared for or even liked!

A child can feel 'inauthentic' and can look for a 'behavioral hideout' a place that he has constructed to give himself safety. Four types of behaviors seem to emerge within the child to protect his self

- **Avoidance:** the young boy withdraws, often at first under the bedcovers, or in daydreaming, overeating, etc.
- **Passive:** the young boy often stumbles upon or finds ways of making himself feel better to avoid the pain, to numb the feelings.
- **Aggressive:** the young boy learns to keep the pain givers 'at bay' by shouting louder, being more verbally, physically or emotionally mean or cruel, becoming 'better' than them through a sophisticated labyrinth of intellectual cleverness, getting bigger and throwing his weight around or generally a doggedness that makes those around him recoil or withdraw.

- **Compliant:** the young boy tries to make things better by agreeing, being good or being everything for everyone. 'If he is good all will be well.'

Most males with drug and alcohol issues that I have worked with developed avoidance behaviors to protect themselves. Of course, not all avoiders end up with a drug or alcohol problem or addiction. This leads us to the next chapter.

Chapter 4

Protective Defenses

Protective defenses are barriers, walls, shells and façades or sealed-off areas within one. They are behavioral patterns we have learned in order to avoid undue stress. They are ways we have learnt to resist or prevent aggression or attack. We develop the basic protective defensive patterns we use throughout our life, very early in life.

What we figure out in childhood for our survival, we continue to do. Our protective defenses are played out over and over again. Whenever any similar pain is triggered, the automatic, 'safe' behavior is put into action. The behavioral patterns are extremely limited and we find ourselves repeatedly going into one of our safe boxes (protective defensive behaviors).

Protective defenses can also be behaviors or beliefs adopted by a person to conceal the true condition(s) pertaining to him or his beliefs. Or they can conceal how he truly thinks and feels. They are a means of self-defense designed to keep from being psychically attacked.

A man can move into a protective-defensive state quickly. In a protective-defensive state, he needs to keep himself in a known, predictable safe way of being in the world.

There are many protective defenses that men use. What I have often found, though, is that the most commonly used protective defenses by men who have come to see me have been: rationalizing and intellectualizing, denying, projecting, regressing, isolating and compensating.

Rationalizing and intellectualizing

This is where a man uses a convincing, logical explanation for his behavior, feelings or decisions, rather than having an awareness of his feelings, impulses or needs. Most men seem to have highly developed this protective defense.

Women often feel very inadequate in communication with men who rationalize and intellectualize in the absence of expressing their feelings. The frustration that women feel often has them calling us for relationship counseling because of 'communication problems' in their relationship.

Denying

Suppressing an awareness of people, events or consequences that could arouse anxiety or pain. The man just says it did not happen. Effectively the man just keeps anything unpleasant out of his everyday consciousness.

Men often say they 'just don't know what happened'. They 'thought everything was going great' until their partner suddenly left them or asked them to leave. For years they may not have wanted to admit that they were not getting their needs met in a relationship.

Regression

This is where a man is overwhelmed by stressful feelings and retreats to a behavior that he relied on (usually) in childhood to help cope with the anxiety. The most frequently presented forms of regression are withdrawing or anger (temper tantrums).

In my work with couples, there can be so much hurt, fear and anxiety that is being experienced by both that it can sometimes be like working with two very young, hurt, angry children. At this point, a lot of protective defenses can be put into place, like denial, isolation, projection.

Projection

Projection is when a man attributes negative feelings, behaviors, faults or limitations to someone or something else that really belong to him. For example, a man might blame his partner for being critical when it is really the man that is criticizing his partner. The classic line used in such circumstances is 'You make me feel'.

Three men wrote of their protective defenses in the context of criticism, blame, sarcasm, and accusation.

Adam

When I receive criticism, blame, sarcasm or accusation from someone that has some sort of power over me (partner, parents, superiors at work) I almost immediately feel like a child. I feel weak, vulnerable, not good enough, failure. I get a feeling of powerlessness and impotence and I am unable to do or succeed. I get a feeling of unworthiness and that I should go away. I go in search of affirmation to pump myself back up.

If I don't think it's my fault I feel badly done by and tend to sulk. Then, after my initial reaction, or if I receive criticism, blame, sarcasm or accusation from someone who doesn't have 'power' over me, I lash out and attack through anger or sarcasm or justifying my position or belittling them.

Howard

All affect me similarly. If I feel there is an element of truth then I am less than perfect.

Martin

I listen to it in the belief that I might learn if it is presented in a soft manner. I don't listen to it if is presented in anger. I withdraw, become empty inside, and feel disconnected, very alone, unsafe and fearful. I listen to it; try to see it as real or unreal about either a situation or myself. How I react is dependent on who does it (e.g., a friend commenting is different from a boss). It hurts me the majority of the time, and depending on the level of fatigue, I react with anger if very tired. If well, I give tit for tat. Basically, it hurts me and I defend myself.

Isolation

When a man separates the link between the mind and feelings to such an extent that his feelings are denied or no longer felt.

Compensation

This is where a man relieves his anxiety by covering up feelings of unacceptance, disapproval, rejection, weakness or limitation by diverting attention elsewhere. A man may become a super worker to make up for and ward off any feelings of inadequacy.

Once protective defenses are the primary experience of living, men can get stuck in behavioral patterns that keep them in a limited way of living their lives. It's like playing snakes and ladders – you keep going down the one path with very little choice. The old patterns draw you down. The snake draws you down, then, later you use the ladders to bring you back up again only until the next time when the snake brings you down once more.

The safe, behavioral protective-defense patterns, such as those just presented, can basically be broken up into three categories:

- **AVOID (Withdraw):** where we cut ourselves off by drinking, drugs, sleep, denial, repression, suppression and other forms of behavior which dissociate us from the world around us and provide us with one in which we feel is more known and safe.
- **COMPLY (Agree/Passive):** when we agree, try to be 'the same', go along with.
- **DOMINATE (Control):** this is a way of controlling our reactions and overriding our protective defenses by using verbal, physical or other forms of manipulation to disempower what we feel is going to overpower us if we do not dominate.

So often, in working with men, it seems they decided as young boys to protect and defend themselves, using whatever behaviors it took to protect themselves with behaviors that went along this continuum.

Avoid/ Withdraw	Comply/ Agree/Passive	Dominate/ Control
Such as • Don't Care • Numb • Plenty of rest • I don't know • Hide • Become invisible • Stay busy	*Such as* • To give • To be good enough • To go along with • Please others	*Such as* • Do it myself • Get attention • Not rely on anyone • Success • Anger

By the time men reach adulthood, they seem encased, preventing them from being in an openly expressive and loving relationship. By their own admission, they need to keep their protective-defense shells around themselves. Women, then, seem to take on the task of cracking them out of their protective-defensive shells.

The protective shells serve men and have allowed them to not just survive, but also utilize these barriers to their advantage and success. Without the protective defenses, men feel naked in the world and too vulnerable for survival.

The problem is that in order for men to be in an intimate relationship, men need to be vulnerable. The paradox, of course, is that the very protective defenses that men used for their survival keep them from being vulnerable and prevent them from experiencing intimacy in relationship. Being vulnerable together is often considered the ultimate intimacy experience.

The barriers (protective defenses) obviously start when life starts (in early childhood). When the child experiences that there is a system out there that he does not understand or could be threatening to him, he begins to layer himself with these protective defenses.

What does it feel like to be behind these protective defenses and what is it like to spend a lifetime behind them? As you read the men's expressions in this book you will begin to get an idea of the protective defenses. For now, imagine being behind so many layers and façades that if someone asked you 'Who are you?' you would have no idea of what layer you were speaking from. More critically, you would have no idea of what they meant by '*you*' in the statement, 'Who are *you*?'

Protective defenses and relationships

Now imagine, years later, that you are in a relationship and a woman is asking you 'How do you feel?' Through layers of façades you can no longer access the feelings and hence are left with only feelings of inadequacy and not good enough (which ironically were the feelings that originally started the layering process). So, what you do is intellectualize, rationalize, philosophize and give what you think, rather than what you feel, or give what you think 'she wants to hear'.

A couple of issues can eventually add to a crisis build up.

1 *Health suffers because of the tension and stress that is internalized.*

2 *The unexpressed, suppressed feelings build up and are often expressed in rage.*

3 *Men are further driven out into the external world to succeed (requiring even more defenses), leaving, yet again, their inner*

world unknown, untraveled, unexperienced and certainly, unexpressed.

4 *The women, if they continue to knock on the façade, become frustrated and angry, and may go on the journey of trying to find 'the right man'.*

Many males, at this time, go looking for a 'more understanding' partner. Something interesting happens at this point. The new 'surrogate' partner listens and a woman begins thinking and saying things like 'I finally found a balanced guy'. The man talks into the night about feelings (usually how he thinks about feelings and usually only up to that level or, perhaps, a few levels into the façade).

Because of this 'semi-catharsis' expression of these layers, many women believe that at last they have found a male who can feel and express who they are. However, within a short time, the layers go back up because the vulnerable part (the young part) of the male needs the *safety* of the protective defenses.

For many women, at this point, they have a sense of 'What happened to love? Where did love go? What happened to our loving relationship? What happened to the magic?'

It is not unusual for women to withdraw, particularly sexually, at this time and many males want to increase the sexual activities at this time to 'feel'. A very familiar polarization begins and the gulf widens.

At this point, because the man has withdrawn again behind his protective layers, he can offer no empathy regarding the woman's emotive outbursts. He has literally 'gone dead', except for outbursts of rage and further sexual releases.

Defense choices

The process of packing up the emotional suitcases continues to occur until there is very little left that resembles a loving relationship. Defenses now are up on both sides. There seem to be about four choices at this time.

1 *Stay in this polarized state; living separate lives with occasional theatrical outbursts to relieve the tension (and to create some feeling). (Many couples are unable to part because of the negative bonding that brought them together in the first place.)*

2 *Leave and continue the pattern with another person.*

3 *Avoid relationships.*

4 *Work through the defenses.*

The 'failure' of another relationship will often lead to further layers of protective defenses, most notably having someone to *blame* for a relationship breakdown. Males often present with what appears to be steel armor around their hearts by the age of 50. The positive side of such a crisis is that if it is big enough it can blow the armor to bits. This leaves the man extremely free and, of course, extremely vulnerable. (More on this in the next chapter under stages and crisis points in a man's life.)

So, it seems as the child grows, he gets hurt, feels pain, experiences the wound and develops protective defenses (barriers, walls, shells, sealed-off areas within himself) to keep himself safe. A man then needs the façade and finds it difficult to survive without it. As the years go by, the 'authentic Self' slips further and further away. To gain confidence, the young man needs to focus on what he is *doing* and what he *has*, because who he *is*, is lost to him. Then, when he grows up, that safe place that has been created keeps others from getting in and him from getting out.

A young man's confidence can often be precarious because it depends on approval, acceptance and success. Later on, in a relationship, when there is pressure to show up more authentically, the young man is in a dilemma. Who he is has been safely sealed away and lost to his conscious awareness. In front of him may be someone demanding that he express what he cannot *see, sense* or *feel.* This usually leads to feeling *shame* in not being able to get it right. This further thickens the walls, making him want to retreat even more. Reactions such as a sense of hopelessness, depression, having an affair or a mid-life crisis can have their origins from this experience.

Chapter 5

Stages of Life
Cycles, Seasons and Tides

Men examining their lives can see an accumulation of unresolved issues that they take from one or more stages of their lives into the next stage of life. Recurring patterns of thought, feelings, body memories and behaviors are shared in the examples that follow.

Teenage years

The typical joke is that a male teenager is a walking, eating hormone. It is a time for the male to tackle the forces of the sexual, sensual and physical energy and his 'spiritual' energy 'spiritual' in this context being reference to what inspires him. Young men in their trial and error experience in relationships can find themselves fusing with females in ways that are confusing and can lead to feelings of overwhelming vulnerability.

The 20s

Ah, yes! What a time! It usually is full steam ahead with very little recognition or appreciation of the details of life. If doubts come up they are quickly dealt with. However, if a man is in a relationship during his 20s, he can be torn between accomplishing in the outside world and attending to the inner world of relationship. Not uncommonly, men choose the outer world.

The vulnerable middle years

The time of life when we face our life and address issues such as:

- Where we have been, are, and where are we going?
- What have we done, are doing, and what do we want to be do and become?
- Who have we been with, are with, and may want to be with?
- What do we do, have, and want?
- What have we accomplished, are accomplishing, and still want to accomplish?
- What do I do about this sense of time running out?
- Why are we here? What is the purpose of life?

These are the kind of questions that men grapple with somewhere between 35 and 50 and beyond, sometimes many times during these years and often in many different ways. The questioning in men's lives may even come in different forms. For example, they can feel confused, fed up, feel they need a change, or feel bored, find themselves daydreaming about, 'What if?' with lots of possible endings, none of which seems to match what they are presently experiencing.

And sometimes men questioning their lives starts as a result of a **crisis** due to a **loss**: of a relationship (parents, friends, partners, family members), their health, their job or even just a sense of their well-being. The death of a parent, particularly, can trigger a lot of unresolved feelings for the son. But, no matter what form the **dissatisfaction** comes in, it is an indication that it is time to review their lives and to see what is really important.

Men at this vulnerable middle time of their lives often start saying things like:

- *"I'm confused."*
- *"I love you, but I'm just not 'in love with you'."*
- *"I just don't know anymore."*
- *"I used to feel so confident, so sure of what I was doing, what I wanted, where I was heading."*
- *"I just feel I want some time and space."*
- *"I don't feel that anyone understands me."*
- *"Things that used to seem important to me, now don't."*

Or their questioning may come in the form of **having fantasies** of being with other women, in other jobs, in different locations (in the country if they are in the city, being overseas, anywhere, other than where they are). Or the fantasies (**daydreaming**) may come regretfully or resentfully in ***'if only'*** thought forms such as: "If only I had: got a better education, had a different wife, did what I really wanted to do, hadn't got myself trapped in a family, found someone who really enjoyed sex the way that I would like it." This mix could also include being torn with a deep sense of family

All these types of experiences indicate that it is time for a change. What men do at this time of life to bring about change can often make a significant difference in their lives; metaphorically, heading out into the desert for years (maybe the rest of their lives) feeling lost, disconnected, nothing is ever quite 'it', OR heading into the next phase of life where they experience generating, creating new ways ***'of being'*** and letting go of *beliefs, values* and *behaviors* that no longer serve them.

Going into ***creation*** rather than ***destruction*** (or **pro-action** rather than **reaction**), allows men to experience life feeling more *connected* (to the Self, others and the greater picture), feeling more *secure* and more *mature*, with a greater sense of *self-accomplishment, self-acceptance* and *self-approval*. This can seem like a hell versus nirvana experience or a sense of chaos versus the blissful (albeit, sometimes fleeting) experience of just enjoying being here, right now. No need to wait to see how the story ends, or even what possibly happens beyond. They get to truly ***experience life***. Using their ***will, determination, intention*** and ***choice*** is their greatest challenge. The ways they utilize these aspects is what will make the difference.

Often how men react during this time may be to have an affair, dump their wife, quit their job, become depressed or get ill.

The 'younger woman syndrome' may also strike him. This is where the man searches for the younger woman. This process involves the non-acceptance of his aging, not wanting to give up his youthfulness, becoming more fascinated with the firm young skin of the body. Wanting, by association with the young firm female, to feel accepted by her and so feel as though he has not lost his own youth, firmness, energy. It could also be a non-acceptance of his fat, sagging skin tucked into clothes that don't quite 'suit' him. Or he may find 'suits' (costumes) that hide it all. Alternatively, his health and looks may become like an obsession with him as he fights off an inevitable process.

When men are confronted by this energy the inclination is usually symptomatic of his having lost access to the younger, feminine part of himself that he gave up to 'make it' in the task-oriented, highly evaluative, competitive masculine world of doing and action, probably to the exclusion of the feminine part of him, which is the being and receiving.

As you read through the views of men about cycles, seasons and tides in their lives, I invite you to form a picture of each man's interpretation of where they have been, where they are at and what is likely for them in the future, without assessment or judgment and seeing what you experience.

Eric

Winter is the season where I am: (1) awaiting the next growth spurt; (2) alone on a personal/intimate level (my contacts with others is as desired); (3) in the middle of winter, or approaching spring but not cold; and (4) I'm quite warm inside and out but there is a temperature that reminds me of winter. All this keeps me looking after and caring for myself.

In terms of the tide, I'm on the incoming tide, just after the wave, because: (1) it is starting to happen; (2) nourishment and support is abundant; (3) the waves are 'fuller' and not dumping on the sand as hard. The water is less murky; and (4) it is not full moon, so not expecting flood tides.

Francis

I am now going into spring. I thought I had been in spring, but it was really a deep, cold, blistering dark winter. Only the realization of this enabled me to enter spring and I am connecting again with Self. I am now better able to connect with my partner and baby son.

I have a realization that today's events still trigger feelings from the past. I have to be in touch with it as my adult self, and not hide from it by distancing, withdrawing, over-reacting. I realize that after all the years at university; I am doing something I don't want to do.

But I can do what I want. It takes action, more study and effort. So I am in spring – a re-growth. However, to get here, I had to go into the dark depths of winter.

Greg

I'm in a Melbourne winter/spring. One minute the sun shines. Life is great; the next is snow and rain. The next there are flowers and the trees have blossomed. There is little consistency both in my emotional and physical feeling as I come to grips with myself and grapple with how I feel and how others make me feel.

Once I was very clear on what my goals were, what I wanted to be. However, I am now not so clear. I have changed in what I want and where I want to be in 10, 20, 30 years.

Howard

My life has four elements: spiritual, physical, emotional and intellectual. As my growth continues as a man this time around I travel to the center of my existence and learn the middle path: sometimes in pain at others in joy. I know these flow together as a tune or song line, a high now will surely change to a low tomorrow and vice versa. I struggle for equanimity and self-acceptance in each and all.

So where am I in my seasons? I am in late spring for spirituality. An awakening has occurred and a model now exists that I follow and that I understand. Surrendering to this path is my challenge. The center or homecoming will be joy, love and connectedness.

Physical aspects of my life have been in dormant winter for many years. I now perceive these fallow years to have been self-imposed. Escape from the chills of winter is to just do things: walk, diet, cycle, make love, all with enjoyment and abandonment to the activity itself and not to fear or be held back by the concept of failing.

Emotional aspects are again in spring bloom, feeling, smelling, touching, seeing, tasting my life are sensed at a high previously held suppressed because of the expectations of others in not showing tears and shouts. Fears, rejection and anger are now being released and mixed with those of joy and laughter of the Cosmic Joke.

Intellectual aspects are in the full growth of summer. All seeds now bear the fruit of the hard work, persistence, experience and knowledge. Complacency, arrogance and intellectual control are my potential nemesis. Developing humility and teaching my truth to others is my salvation.

Ivan

At this very time I feel I am getting to know my wife. I wonder why I didn't get to know her before, but I think it's because when I met my wife we had limited time together. I was in business working hard and my initial time with my wife was limited because she was already a mother of three.

So I look back now and think I was trying to get to know all four people and making them part of my life. I just thought as long as I am a husband and do what a husband does, and do what a father does, I would be OK – do my duty.

It seems now I look back I've been an OK father, but I know that my wife and I fell in love and have survived on that feeling of being in love ever since, without fulfilling each other's needs. All our children have left home now, we have four grandchildren that come and stay, and I am now mature enough to read their faces and thoughts whereas I was too busy before, and, by the way, we get to hand them back to their parents, which leaves my wife and I alone again. Initially when the children left, or rather the last one left (this year) my wife and I had trouble talking; we were trying to think of things to say to each other so the place/house wasn't so quiet. Now I am inquisitive about my wife. I am appreciating her more as a person I can see more of her personality now and I am absorbing every bit I can.

I've got a fair way to go still, but I'm working on it. It's like taking three steps forward and two back all the time. I seem to have done most things in reverse. I've had grandchildren at age 33 and experienced their babyhood, had young children at the age 24, and adults (as children) in my early 30s. But at age 42 I now almost feel equipped to be a father to my children. I love my wife differently now and it appears to be varying all the time.

If men have not looked at themselves, and they decide they want to examine their lives later in life, it can be very difficult to break through the walls. The defenses are stronger.

They can be so afraid by the time they are in their 50s to be caught out because it could invalidate who they are, how they identify themselves and what they have been involved with for the past 50 or so years.

To bring about change is so exciting for the person and the therapist as well. It is almost as if you can see chains falling to the ground. It is not uncommon to hear the cries, the murmurs when the defenses break away.

One of the biggest worries for men is how they are going to function in their external world now that their feelings are exposed. The vulnerability of the child re-emerges. The vulnerability that was so pressing as a child.

At this time in therapy it is so important to talk about balance and how to be appropriate with their feelings. It is generally observed that in western countries, when a man cries, he is still criticized – one of his worst fears!

We are all familiar with men who, in their 50s, take on a younger woman hoping to recapture their own youthfulness. This is often an attempt (usually unconscious and denied) to go back in time and reconnect with the unresolved lost feminine ('the feeling part') aspect of themselves. Men's soft feelings can only be experienced with someone who is soft. Men have often related that they feel most vulnerability when they are with someone else who is vulnerable.

When a man looks at the partner of his own age, he may be reminded of his own aging process. This could be enough for him to seek a more youthful partner as a reflection of himself. (We need to remind ourselves that the greatest number of separations/divorces occur with people in their 50s around what is sometimes referred to as 'the empty nest syndrome'.)

Then there is the developmental reality of aging and dying parents and the adolescent children or young adults attempting to separate out from the man in his 50s. He is neither here nor there. There is no place for him, it seems.

This can be a very despairing time for a man as he looks forward and sees how life ends and looks back and views the 'mistakes' he has made in the past. He can also be faced with the issues of aging, loss, if both parents are deceased the realization that there is no one between him and death or childhood hurts from needs that still have not been met. Any or all of these and other issues can be revisited and positively reframed and a man can enter into this stage of life experiencing his wisdom, renewed energy and the confidence from knowing that the answers lie within. And a more constant state of bliss can come from the gentle act of surrender and a sense of true acceptance in experiencing what feels like a more authentic self.

Chapter 6

Men in Relationships

Most men have expressed being hurt, bruised or put down in some way in childhood. Because of experiences like this, they tell of having developed a false sense of themselves (the development of protective defenses, presented earlier). The protective defenses keep them safe and secure until they enter a relationship.

We are not taught much about relationships. We just observe and battle through. Sooner or later we do make a decision whether we are going to comply, avoid or dominate in relationships. One of the fallouts is that men can find themselves on the cold outer and women are perplexed and hurt by the indifference. Another effect can be that the man distances himself from the experiential world of his feelings and embraces the safety and security of the rational mind. Some women have expressed views to me like, 'Men walk around like ice cubes daring to be melted and fiercely avoiding the heat that could contribute to the warming and softening'.

Another metaphorical way of viewing this is that after years of protecting themselves from being hurt by building higher and thicker walls (made of rational masonry) that keeps others out and themselves locked in, men lose sight of understanding and their inner world.

And when women want more, men (because they have lost sight of themselves) feel unacceptable. They seem to have forgotten about that part of themselves that women want (referred as the 'Self' throughout the book). Women want men to be intimate and to share their inner lives. Men don't feel safe doing this, and many men have no idea of what this is even about.

The one major way that men try to enter into the women's world is to enter (have sex with) the women, to sexualize their feelings. If men don't feel they cannot get hurt further. Of course, there is not much joy in the relationship based just on sex, without feelings, passion, interest, excitement and a common sense of purpose (an inspirational connection).

In a relationship, men's partners want (almost demand) to know who they are. Most men do not *understand* the questions because their authentic Self went into hiding. It went underground (unconscious) to make room for the protective defenses.

Watch what you experience as you read what some of the men expressed about their experience of relationships.

Jessie

The hardest thing in a relationship for me is to be vulnerable and trusting and to have a prolonged period of intimacy. It's as if, when everything is going well, when joy, trust and love abounded, I need to pull back from the edge to withdraw from the commitment. This is if it becomes intolerable to be in a relationship that is so joyful and beautiful.

Kent

The most difficult aspect of a relationship for me is the expectation that my partner should be perfect in every way, even though I know that it just can't be so. I suppose that it is my own desire for a perfect world that I seek perfection in my partner. I want my partner to be the source of all my satisfaction, the cure of all my ills. I want my relationship to be easy, and I want my partner to not be just who she is but to possess every desirable aspect of every other woman.

My difficulty in a relationship stems from viewing my relationship from what is not there, rather than living the marvelous experiences that I share with my partner.

Lester

Rejection and the betrayal of trust are, for me, what it is like being in relationship and is the way I know myself in the world. Relationships are like a mirror of paradoxes. It is like love, a projection of all aspects of myself. I don't always get what I expect (perhaps we never, in the end, get what we expect). Perhaps when I let go into this, I get more than I expect. Without having a relationship I cannot know myself. Without rejection I cannot grow.

As a small child I felt at the center of my/the world. Gradually through my parents' criticism and rejection I grew to know that I am only a small part of things. I have started on my journey towards grace and individuation. Without relationships and their failure I could not do this. Relationships are the boat I travel in, over and through the sea of the spirit.

Martin

The hardest thing in relationships for me is not being heard, which is the wider aspect of not actually ever been seen for myself and allowed to be myself both positive and negative. In dealing with women the pain of watching them attack not because of what has occurred between us but rather their failure to control or mold me into what they think I should be. It is also difficult for me to see through what I see as the artifice, image or front of women's words and actions to discern, love and respect the 'real' them.

The lack of honesty and the desire to maintain beliefs without questioning whether they are accurate hurts, as well as the cowardice at real confrontation and vulnerability as women busily protect themselves. The feeling of being used or being seen as an object, not someone who is loved and respected for Self but rather something to be used and discarded.

Rejection hurts but the above manner of rejection hurts most because it never gives a chance at reconciliation of the pain between people and leaves open wounds. Criticism hurts but does not wound provided it is fair and constructive and not meaning to wound. Women don't fight fair but expect or demand that men fight fair and protect them but only when they choose. This double standard leaves out honesty and hurts everyone.

Noel

The hardest thing to deal with in relationships for me is to be caught up in the ongoing argument that comes with the assumption of archetypal roles. This might seem a contradiction because even being in a relationship is playing these roles.

Certainly, criticism and rejection are lurking around and highlighting my fears. But in dealing with the projections that come from my partner and in dealing with the projections that I give to my partner the greatest loss for me is the loss of INTIMACY.

I feel that when I am caught up in the process of conflict I have lost contact with myself and am made powerless by it. I also know that I am dealing with some of my unresolved issues in this process and I have to go through to their resolution. I just wish I could go straight to it get in touch with my feelings and express my fears.

From my work with men over the years they have expressed that they are scared (terrified would probably be more accurate) of speaking openly and honestly with women because of a number of possible factors:

1 Their experience of being with overly-demanding mothers (in the absence of their fathers).

2 The absence of a role model (father) who would assist them in transforming bewildering experiences, not only in their own father, but also in men, generally.

3 Their need to be the responsible gender, mixed with their fear of being criticized and not getting it right. Reading through the 'Criticism, Sarcasm, Blame and Accusation' sections of the men speaking certainly highlights men's vulnerability.

4 Their despair and being overwhelmed in being so responsible for the wrongs that have occurred, as put forward by those who claim that men have been the source of violence, cruelty, lack of feeling and inability to express themselves. At the very best, the average man would probably be confused about how he should be and behave, what his priorities should be and how to be present in a personal relationship. Most men appear to give in to the opinion of women regarding their behavior. They then blame the women for why they lead secret, unexpressed lives.

Rationing Love

Different people find their own ways of rationing their love. So many men in *The Men's Group* reported that their experience was 'If you give your all, it can leave you feeling incredibly hurt and vulnerable.'

Men have expressed that when they ration their love they do it by withholding their thoughts and feelings because they might not be accepted if expressed. What men tend to do is overly express in a physical way to compensate for not knowing, or being afraid to express feelings or thoughts. Men look loving and giving, but if they are feeling not good enough their flurry of activity and doing things keeps up their façade and morale. They learn that if they stay busy enough, they do not have to address what they think or feel. When they stop, their feelings of inadequacy and lack of success creep in and they can get down, feel a sense of emptiness, or depleted, with nothing more to give. At times like this they report that they start rationing their love.

In therapy sessions, what men speak is that mostly the mother raised them in the absence (physical, emotional, psychological, spiritual or ritual) of the father.

What the young boy seems to experience is that the male with whom he is to identify is not present. The female is (overly) present. The boy, logically, very likely could draw a number of conclusions from this experience.

1 Men are not there and women are disappointed.

2 Women (the mother) want the son to be what his father (her partner) is not. Namely, there, attentive, interactive and providing for her needs.

3 Women (the mother) are never quite satisfied with the male, making excuses for his absences, or openly criticizing him, covertly lamenting his loss, or finally getting fed up and physically separating from him.

4 The boy sees that he is male (like his father); therefore, he must be like his father and incur the disappointment of his mother, or be unlike his father (and more like his mother) in order to get on with a woman.

5 In the absence of his father, a 's-mothering' can take place whereby the boy has to be the emotional (and sometimes, intellectual, social, even physical through hugs, kisses and other forms of physical contact) support for his mother.

And these types of conclusions, related by men over the years, are just the conclusions of what is typically called a 'normal' family. Add in other factors, such as physical, verbal, psychological, emotional or sexual abuse, and the conclusions drawn about who the boy is as a male and how he should act as a man are usually intensified and deepened into protective defenses. Often these protective defenses are creatively and charmingly hidden.

All of this is happening within the experience of 'being in love' with the mother.

Take Quincy. He presented as a good-looking charming, charismatic man. He had developed a way of being and presenting himself in the world through his speech, dress, mannerisms and social talents that endeared him to both men and women.

Quincy first came to see me at the age of 29 (about to turn 30) in a crisis state. (The odds are that he would experience another crisis state at around 39.) Quincy was typical of a son with an absent father. His father, an alcoholic, was absent both emotionally and physically. His mother was a larger than life, strong, determined woman who focused on her two boys, Quincy being the oldest. His mother fashioned the two boys to be just what the father was not.

Quincy responded to the coaching by his mother and grew up to be just what the mother wanted, but not his Self. The mother took great delight in going out on 'dates' with her son and experiencing great pleasure and pride when entering a restaurant with the polished product – her son. (Quincy, at the time, was a cook.)

The first crisis Quincy discussed with me was when the (very successful, strong, powerful) woman he was dating became pregnant. Just several days before his 30th birthday, Quincy felt totally overwhelmed and 'consumed' by the pressure of the impending imprisonment with the (personification of his mother) woman.

At this time, he was a party person, lots of drinking, smoking, party drugs, late nights, night jobs (in restaurants, his home turf). He was an absolutely charming man! Look at how Quincy views himself in relationships.

Quincy

There are a few things I find difficult. One is being a question of tenure. Relationships always seem to end on me usually quickly. Then start afresh with a blaze of hope and glory, thence petering out in the usual manner. It seems I go into relationships with unspecified intentions and little expectations.

I am also very selfish in relationships. I also get to a certain point where both my Self and my partner are opening up to possibilities, mostly positive, and I either destroy them or am incapable to carry them through. It seems at the point of just before leaving a relationship when I'm in self-questioning mode, I feel helpless, rudderless, completely out of my depth and without any wisdom to rely on (both instilled or experienced). At that point I believe I'm in a very juvenile space. Most times I wish difficulties to arise (and even create them) in order to give me a reason to leave (or mistreat) a relationship.

In what the men wrote on rationing of love, so much of what is expressed comes from previous hurts that brought about fears and crippled their communication. During the MenSpeak section on 'rationing of love', the men who were present during the process expressed that they were surprised how patterns of behavior as children were still evident today in their adult relationships.

Men and their feelings

I often hear women say that men do not express their feelings other than to get very angry or go into a sulk. This appears to be both historical and circumstantial. If men were only taught these two options (anger and sulking which is usually presented as fight and flight, I would add normally *inward*), they experience their own limitations and are frustrated with not being able to adequately express themselves. When they learn to allow the feelings to surface and learn how to appropriately express them they express feelings of immense freedom, inner peace and being truly sure of themselves.

Women often try to make their relationships better by getting closer and having men experience and express their feelings. Because many men cannot access their feelings, they experience *criticism, blame, sarcasm* and *accusation* (forms of projection). Look at the fear of intimacy expressed by Oliver and Parker.

Oliver

I do not think I have ever been totally intimate with my partner. To be totally intimate would be to share everything that I feel. My fears in sharing everything are twofold: (1) it places me totally in my partner's hands, exposed; (2) I am not sure my partner will appreciate/accept all of my feelings as they relate to her.

The other practical reality is that to be intimate my partner must be in touch with her emotions in order to be able to express them. I find this difficult. Intimacy is the lifeblood of a relationship. Without it we cannot go forward together.

Parker

Commitment is for me (based on experience of losses in my life) almost impossible. It hurts me too much when somebody goes away. Intimacy reminds me that I am not good enough, and if I am not good enough a partner they won't like me, and she will go away. And that hurts like hell. I am sorry to myself for being like this and

I pray to a God for my own understanding that this can and will continue to change.

Looking at the behavioral pattern according to the responses of so many of the men, they tended to view how to behave from two options: respond aggressively if they feel they have the power or withdraw/avoid if they feel powerless. Both of these are reactions of the child at different ages.

It is interesting that Howard, age 50, had more options. Initially he still felt overwhelmed, powerless, very young and hurt. He also was able to *"ground myself again in my manhood (adult), get rational thoughts together and choose* [my emphasis] *an appropriate response"*.

With Howard, who had done a lot of individual and group work, he learned more options that led to both resolution of conflict and feeling okay about himself. Howard had developed more skills. He had the ability to *process* and by *'grounding himself back into the adult'* he was able to hold his *'manhood'*, or authentic Self, rather than slipping behind the façade of protective defenses.

Then there is Oliver, age 35, who was just beginning to learn how to identify and express his feelings. He says that criticism, blame, sarcasm and accusation comes like a *'jolt, thud and I get stooped in my posture, muscles hurt, I feel powerless. I fend it off. I don't believe any of it* [cuts himself off, dissociates, compartmentalizes] *until I've had enough and then return same on the same level.'* Oliver is like the child who has learned to give back exactly what he gets. With more personal work, Oliver could learn to trust himself more in having more ways of dealing with various forms of disapproval.

Xavier expresses his compliance, with such poetic expression: *"I first take criticism, blame, sarcasm or accusation on without question. I seem to be a dry sponge just ready to absorb anything that a person, especially a female, may throw at me. In all other areas of my life I would evaluate, consider before accepting; but here I seem to act from automatic and say, 'What have I done? She's right. This is justified'.*

"The first thing I feel is a deep piercing pain, a dagger in the guts, then the heart begins to ache. Then I withdraw, shrivel up, enclosed. But in this state it takes just a further slight or criticism to produce rage. Deep, mad rage, driven by pain. The rage is in words and movement, noise, violence to myself, clenching my jaw, hitting my head against a wall, even beating myself. I have never directed this violence on anyone else but the only thing stopping me is fear of the damage I could do. I thank God I have never gone that far. The pain would be even worse."

First Xavier agrees (complies), internalizes what is given to him and then avoids, with very little sense of choice or chance of growth in this pattern. Xavier practiced expressing and releasing his pain. Even just being able to say how he felt in some way was a great start and relief as he increasingly made decisions that were more in his best interests and not just from pleasing others or being liked.

Chapter 7

Choice Regarding Reactions Criticism, Blame, Sarcasm and Accusation And How We React to Them

Anxiety arises whenever an externally or internally motivated instinct becomes strong enough to arouse conflict. The anxiety reaction recalls the anticipation of punishment and guilt and triggers the protective defensive process.

The protective defensive behaviors channel the energy into action. (As presented in Chapter 3, action, along with task orientation, accomplishment, effort and achievement are the most typical expression of what is referred to as *masculine energy*. This is in contrast to *feminine energy* that expresses itself through the experiences of being open, accepting, allowing, curious. Again, let me emphasize that the terms *masculine* and *feminine energy* should not be confused with male and female. Both men and women can be in *masculine* or *feminine energies*). The actions of men may or may not be acceptable to others, or even to a man's own 'Self'.

As presented in the previous chapter, most coping behaviors are to protect and defend us from a perceived attack or potential pain. Men found themselves incredibly vulnerable to criticism, blame, sarcasm and accusation, especially from female partners.

Howard

Criticism, blame, sarcasm and accusation all affect me similarly. If I feel there is an element of truth then I am less than perfect.

Martin

I listen to it in the belief that I might learn if it is presented in a soft manner. I don't listen to it if is presented in anger. I withdraw, become empty inside, and feel disconnected, very alone, unsafe and fearful. I listen to it; try to see it as real or unreal about either a situation or myself. How I react is dependent on who does it (e.g., a friend commenting is different from a boss). It hurts me the majority of the time, and depending on the level of fatigue, I react with anger if very tired. If well, I give tit for tat. Basically, it hurts me and I defend myself.

The reactions of men were what so many of the men wanted to change. They would often relate stories that included how their behaviors were learned and are now reactive, automatic and habitual responses. The behaviors had to be automatic to enable men to act efficiently when a potential (perceived) threat presented itself. The emphasis, here, is that their protective defenses are automatic.

Most of the protective defenses used by men are outside their own consciousness; that is, men are unaware that they are using them. These reactions disempower men in how they deal with experiences. Men, who look at themselves, do gain insight and practice proactive ways of anticipating and dealing with difficult emotional circumstances that arise in their lives.

The aware man

Men need to understand that their behavioral habits are just that – behaviors and habits that have been developed to protect and defend their selves. The habits are what men ***learned***. The habits are ***not who men are!*** They are ***what men do***, to varying degrees, and behaviors and habits can be changed. Men ***can*** and ***do*** learn how to respond appropriately to the crescendo of environmental and relationship stresses in their lives!

Men can and do learn the importance of reducing stress through a) realistic insights; b) aware, internalized values and beliefs, and c) creative, positive and proactive responses. This is what is meant by men learning how to *process*. The aware man is one who is acting on today's information, responding and pro-acting, rather than relying on habit and memory to guide him.

The aware man is a man who has reviewed his values, beliefs and behaviors and has learned to let go of those that no longer serve him. He has adopted updated values, beliefs and behaviors that are appropriate for his life today. They are not based on what he learned in getting by in previous stages of his life.

A man needs to learn, experience and internalize that he has a unique rational dimension to his functioning. That he has the possibility, no matter how difficult, of taking action that will change and dictate his present and future life. As therapists, we have to work from this premise.

The men I have worked with and who have contributed to this book began, or were well on the journey towards, achieving this. Men who are frustrated in where they are in life, in work and in relationship to a partner, others or their 'Self' have to take up the enquiry for their own physical, psychological, emotional and, I would add, spiritual (what inspires him) well-being.

When we as men are threatened or wounded, the child within us goes heading down the protective-defensive pathway wanting to be safe. In learning to process, we can bring back and center ourselves in our adult. The adult within us will enable us to be proactive, rather than reactive, utilizing the 'Self' to assist him in moving from the reaction of the young, wounded child to the able, insightful adult.

Chapter 8

Who Was I? My Eulogy

I asked the men to write their own eulogy. I introduced the topic with a visualization where they imagined the people who were important in their lives, even in some small way, standing at their graveside. Although the bodies they had inhabited were in a coffin about to be lowered, they too, in some form, were standing with those who have gathered. The powerful cello music of David Darling was playing in the background as the men wrote:

Umar

Umar was a man who like many others, came into being not out of love and in love, but simply due to an 'accident'. That fact had a major impact on his life and colored his perception of who he was and how others viewed him.

He walked around carrying deep wounds and most of all, always eager to play the part that he thought was his to play in life: the selfless helper to others (mother, father, brothers, sister), 'fixer' of his parents problems and marriage and the dumb student at school (because that's what his mother said he was).

He was always searching for love and approval (that he felt he didn't get from his parents) from others. That was who Umar was for many years, despite 'growing up' into a 'man'.

Then a chance to grow came along and to his credit he seized it with both hands (and all his heart), and learnt that, to a large extent, he had been playing someone else's part thinking someone else's thoughts, going through someone else's pain.

With lots of heartache, honest and truth, he learnt that he didn't have to be what he thought he had to be. He could be everything he thought he couldn't (or shouldn't) be! (It was even okay to fuck-up and still be positive about it!)

Umar subsequently went onto blossom into a wonderful, loving, affectionate, peaceful man! Things just got better and better!

He married a sweet girl who was ready and willing to embark on a process of growth that led them to feel emotions that they thought didn't exist, as they had not experienced these emotions (such as intimacy, tranquility or trust) in their respective families.

Umar went on to have a child with his companion and felt good and serene about it because he knew he had given his son the biggest gift of all: he had broken the chain. He would be able to give unconditional love.

Umar died after having achieved in life more than he ever could dream. The man who died was not the same person that was born years ago, because he had realized that change is the most important thing in life and he knew he would be ready to continue his journey in the next life.

Victor

We are gathered here today to say our final farewell to Victor who has died and merged with the light of which he so often spoke.

It is easy to dwell on his achievements, particularly those of the latter half of his life when he contributed so much through his art, his writing and his healing work. But these were only the trace of the man, the mark of his spirit as it moved through this life.

His greatest creation was his own life and the way his spirit touched and uplifted ours.

Deeply committed to his wife and children, he gave selflessly of himself to uplift and encourage their growth, and he received as much love and wisdom from them as he gave.

What we will miss most about Victor are the deeper things that moved through him: his warmth, love and understanding; his active and practical compassion for others; the way he uplifted and inspired those whose lives he touched directly or through his art and writing; his passion about life; his larger-than-life love of life; the exultation and joy that poured through him; his wisdom and insight that he shared so openly with others; his courage in facing the truth about himself; and his living true to his inner, higher self.

Victor, we bid you a swift passage to the home of your spirit.

Holding your memory in our hearts, we thank you for so enriching our lives.

Walter

Walter was a man who loved other people; always found ways to help where there was a need and to give comfort where there was pain.

He was always striving to find ways to share what wisdom he had found himself and show others that life is to be lived and enjoyed. He did this by leading with example, allowing and encouraging anyone who saw the possibilities to join him.

While setting and achieving goals was important to him, he always managed to inject some fun into his work, managing to strike a rare and beautiful balance in life.

To be with Walter often meant making challenges to be accepted and safe ways of doing things, which made his life and lives of those around him a constant adventure. He would not allow himself to be held back by senseless rules or conventions, but did not ignore or devalue the feelings of others.

Walter was a sensitive and open man, unafraid to allow his feelings to be seen. He was a living example of how beautiful, challenging, satisfying and joyous life can be.

Those of us fortunate enough to have been touched by his life will forever count our blessings and in difficult times will be able to think of him and remember not to surrender hope.

Walter showed us that a wondrous and authentic life is not only a possibility, but that we should settle for nothing less.

Xavier

Xavier was a good friend to many.

He was loved by many.

He had both success and failure in his life.

He contributed to the planet, and took from the planet.

He really did have a deep, rich and complex life.

But for all this he was never quite happy with his life.

He often spoke of this 'bottomless pit of desire'.

He attempted to fill it with the love and approval of women: a wife, daughters, lover.

He tried to fill it with the love of friends.

He tried to fill it with the approval of his patients, his neighbors or his peers.

And, of course, all the love and approval in the world were forthcoming, but in those moments of aloneness the pit was absolutely bare.

All the love with universe could not put a tiny dent in this empty space.

I suppose you could say he experienced the angst of existence as the classical existential fool.

His greatest regret was that he took it all so seriously.

He looked so hard, missed so much lightness.

He was so intent on digging, on probing, on analyzing, on learning, that sometimes he felt that he had missed it all... missed all the light and laughter, and dwelt in the valley of the shadow of death.

His death must be familiar territory.

When the men spoke of the baffling or profound (such as death, spirit, soul, the meaning of life or love) the range of what they imagined seemed pretty normal and based mostly on what they were taught.

But as I sat in the circle listening, I was always struck by the sheer poetry, deep emotion, and extraordinary sense of connection to themselves and others in not so much what they believed but in their expression. Maybe it was the fact that the men wrote their elegiac thoughts one at a time, sentence by sentence, pausing, then adding some more that the eulogies took on poetic form, appearance and expression. This was what I longed to be part of when the circle of men met. This is what I miss.

Chapter 9

The Spiritual Man Experience

The men speaking of being spiritual was for me some of the most lyrical, insightful, and connected experiences of what they spoke and wrote.

With what it meant to experience being a spiritual man, my task was to invite the men into the world of possibilities that included such possibilities as: whatever it is that we are, is what is not there when we are (so called) dead!

Some were comfortable and even embraced the powerful world of the spirit, soul, essence, life force, eternal dreamtime or energy. Others allowed themselves, in the absence of truly knowing, to enter through the door of their imagination and allow their selves to experience their spiritual man.

Ralph

When I get out of my own way and allow myself to be, I often experience a sensation, an insight, calmness, a self-expansion and freedom of movement. This quite different experience of myself is so energizing and exhilarating, I really get a sense of my own power, potential, and I say, 'Goodness, if only I felt like this more often, for longer periods, so much more could happen for me'. These brief times of experiencing my greater than usual Self often occur after meditation, looking deeply within, letting go of the common guides of my daily life.

Moon, stars, cloudy sky, to the heavens I reach.
How much further to find my peace?

O how great is the heavens where gods reside and wisdom waits.

O how much I long to be there and now I know my spirit waits.

Harmony springs forth like artesian water hot and bubbly from the depths of me.

How hard I've worked to taste the wine, the blend of struggles of such a time.

Connectedness with others, with Self, what a wonderful flow that comes and goes.

With all humanity I do share the hope and love that our souls will meet.

Being myself without the fear (it wears me down) but I really need to say that this for me is the only way.

My own strength scares me too but onward soldier I will go.

When I feel the love within me I know my spirit awakens each time. Like a newborn baby it cries aloud, striving to find its feet. At first like a ship it floats around destination unknown, but it has an anchor and love is known.

Scott

My spiritual man comes alive when I step out of my immersion in day-to-day activities and experience a sense of perspective. It is when I detach from my learned responses and observe myself responding, not just reacting. It is when I feel pleasure or happiness or sadness, anxiety, frustration and acknowledge these. It is listening to a jazz piece and marveling at the resonance of an apparently dissonant chord. It is absolute sense of perfection when I am skiing fast and I make a long sweeping turn on my edges, smoothly, crisply, minimum effort but feeling like I am on a rail; the absolute balance of body/mind/snow/skis; the feel of the surface beneath, the fluidity of my movements; the feeling that it doesn't get much better than this.

It is the sense of nothingness sometimes, just sitting and being aware of my body.

My spirit, the 'me energy', is the way I can touch people's lives. It is when I can observe them as a totality with comfortable and uncomfortable aspects and with their own reality. It is when I can experience their reality and feel their reality. It is when I let them touch me with their spirit.

Tim

To be a spiritual man is the acceptance of something greater than me as a worker, provider, and macho image. This acceptance of the spirit is a sense of freedom and a feeling of surrender. I sense freedom because my spirit is not demanding, never judgmental and allows me to enter into a peaceful space, a place that is deeply calming with a unique completeness as if it has taken all my characteristics and put them into absolute balance. A feeling of surrender for me is also representative of me giving up, letting go of the normal world and inviting into me a new level, a new dimension of existence. By surrendering I feel I have been given more power to a balance in my life.

To express myself spiritually is to accept others without judgment, and to contribute to others genuinely with no thought of gain. As this develops, my connection with my Self and others becomes clearer with a sense of simplicity and peace. It's as if the spirit is already satisfied and seeks nothing from anyone nor demands anything of myself. There is then a real freedom to genuinely express myself with a feeling of love.

Chapter 10

Summary and Suggestions

In keeping with how this book came about, each reader who graciously and generously gave of their time to provide feedback on ***MenSpeak*** were also asked to briefly provide their impressions on what was most valuable for them and any further suggestions for others who will read this book. Just using the primary sources and not outside references has been continued in the summary and suggestions.

To be an aware man requires the courage to responsibly enjoy life so that others walk into the worthwhile peaceful world you have created.

Too often, there is a space in the heart that closes up, just as sure as locking a door. The reward for closing the heart is that we appear more rational, without the interference and the unpredictability of emotions. The rational mind becomes stronger and then it dominates. Balance is lost. Usually, then, an external focus reassures that we are okay, that we are lovable, acceptable, approvable and successful.

For some men, and for all who aspire to be in the male spirit, this external focus can be expressed in business, finance, politics and power. The energy that pushes us to be creative and acknowledged can also take the form of being initiators or elders in a community of alternatives. This external focus for life is seductive. In time, we can become addicted to the external experience of the lives we create to feel worthwhile. Fear can then become our motivation for continuing with what we have created, through the fear of 'losing it' as our only, or primary identification.

A lot of sexual expression emanates from a closed heart, and our inability to express our feelings. Because our heart is closed, our inner Self searches for an escape valve to let off some experience of connectedness. This can result in an exploration of a pseudo heart-space through sexual activity. We particularly mourn when we sense that our partner's heart space is also closed. Sometimes, in participating in sexual activity, we seem to know it is not heart felt (by us or our partner).

And yet, sexual expression provides at least some form of connectedness. We may even resist sexual expression if we feel cheated, neglected or abandoned by the experience. The male spirit feels the pain. It feels the wounded heart. A pained, wounded heart can often have the physical manifestation of viewing a man in a state of nothingness, staring into space (and sometimes at another goddess) hoping to be rescued from darkness, deadness and automaticity. Longed for is to experience the light, to be alive and to create.

The heart space, if buried or forgotten, can be identified through feelings of being not understood, alone, isolated and existing in a secret world. Sadness occurs. A tragedy has the male spirit gasping and grasping for pleasures that intellectually and physically satiate him. At the same time, loss of connection to a heart-space can leave men bereft of their emotional and experiential Self (what most men allow to be expressed when they are in an 'in love experience').

At a practical level, if these hurts are discussed there is a tremendous clash with the rational mind. The intellect is highly developed as a defense. Breaking through can be so incredibly difficult. It would be like speaking about the possibilities of becoming a bird and flying. The male spirit could easily feel earthed and bewildered, feeling trapped in a body, moving with a slow heaviness. Often the look in men's eyes is saying, 'I understand the words you are saying, but I don't know *how* to change my experience'.

Men's buried memory of the beauty of their emotional Self seems to emerge through the conscious longing for the lightness of the females who touch them in some way. This can lead to needing the feminine energy they connect with and then resenting that they need the female to connect with that energy, and also resenting that they need it at all. This co-dependency has bitterness and resentment as its bartering tool within the male. As it develops, the man can easily get into trying to always 'get it right' with the emergence of needing to get things perfect. But so many men do not seem to know what 'it' is. They hope the lightness of the female will lead them to 'it'. And yet, men get angry when what they thought was lightness turns out to be the unfulfilled needs in the female looking for completion in the male.

Usually it was the pain in the non-relationship the men were having with a partner that brought them to me to seek counseling, either privately or as part of *The Men's Group*. Men tended to present, most often, at the ages of being in their late 20s, 30s, and 40s of their lives and feeling stuck behind the façade before the next decade.

A crime against men is that they have been taught to conceal their feelings. So many men have been shamed in their families by their fathers (when relating to their mothers) and their mothers (when being too much like their fathers), as well as on the streets and playgrounds and in public arenas where sensitivity was not accepted and usually ridiculed. One man in *The Men's Group* said: *'I always hoped that there might be a place where speaking would be so different. On the first day it took such courage just to walk from the car to the door. And what a difference it has made.'*

When men speak, they tend to assess their lives rather than share their experiences. In this book you see how quickly men can move from speaking from the heart to a safer teaching, conceptualizing, philosophizing posture. Sometimes they talk *about* their experience without actually expressing their feelings

In *The Men's Group*, the room would go silent, and a different energy came into the room, a different feeling when a man started speaking from the heart. Sometimes, the men seemed to regress, experiencing how they felt when they were little children. The main purpose of the group was for men to learn ways to 'process' this, understand themselves and make the changes in their lives that brought a sense of wholeness and self-acceptance.

And they all expressed how they felt vulnerable and it is often that vulnerability that stops them from sharing. It stopped them because they wondered how they could function, do their work *and* feel vulnerable. How could they negotiate in meetings, be strong, be with males in the male world, hold their power... if they allowed vulnerability?

When men speak and are really listened to, they are expressive of their feelings. I have experienced this in both individual counselling sessions and group work. What I have found is that men speak when they feel safe. Men also speak when their pain becomes acute and they are in a crisis state.

And men do become more confident in expressing their current (and earlier) hurts and do seek to understand how earlier hurts are connected to their existing experience. In men speaking, they do make new decisions about life that move them in the direction of more expressive and loving relationships with themselves, their partners, their family (of origin and current) and others. Men no longer need to feel shame about their fear of taking a relational risk!

A Brief Snap Shot

Male/female differences

It seems clear that men and women are different. Neither party should try to make their partner more like themselves. It may well be one of the deciding factors that destroy the masculine/feminine balance and ultimately the harmony of the relationship.

Relationships

Good relationships have good communication, involving:

1 Appreciation that men and women use very different ways to communicate.

2 Compassion for our Selves and one another.

3 Understanding that men and women cope with stress and deal with conflict very differently.

4 Having a way of communicating that involves one person speaking and the other just listening (*processing*).

Opening to better communication

- Consider the possibility that we only get this one life to totally enjoy it, give as much to it and get as much from it. Develop a way of speaking that actually gets you what you want, rather than the fallout from not getting what you want because you did not know how to ask. This book is about men speaking, but in a way that is open, frank, vulnerable, strong and direct with a view to having an intimate, deeply spiritual and creative life. Life is about continually becoming more and more authentic. Find even one person or sit in a circle, with men and women speaking truly and honestly being them Selves.

- It is not unusual for couples to come up with a few or a list of renovations in the person they love that would make them even better. And, of course, we are usually with the opinion of the person we are with, rather than the person. This creates differences that can easily turn into a disagreement and lead to argument. It is not that we argue that can hurt, but how we argue. How a person presents their point of view is usually what hurts, not the content or that they have a different opinion. How they speak to each other (I would say from my personal and professional experience) is always what makes the difference. If either party starts speaking to the other from a parental position it deteriorates the loving adult and child-like interactions that are so much more fun and intimate.

Enhancing suggestions for men

For men there are many opportunities for enhancing the male experience.

Be part of a men's group to connect with others going through similar experiences, to express yourself and to process your experiences in a trusted safe space.

Work with a therapist to prevent reliving negative childhood patterns.

Learn how to argue so that the focus after an argument is not on your anger, shouting, or any other offensive and threatening behavior but rather on the content and issue presented.

Find positive ways to reward your Self that does not include unhealthy behaviors such as excessive drinking, smoking, overeating, or engaging in dangerous activities.

PART II
MenSpeak

Part II is the verbatim transcript of what each of the 24 men wrote. The only changes were to any word or statement that could identify them and to arbitrarily change and put into alphabetical order the names of each participant.

I have not included usual background labels of the socio-psycho-economic-calendric-historic-geographic-occupational identifiers we search for in our everyday social or professional exchanges. This is for reasons of both privacy and for allowing the reader to conjure up who each man is based on what he says. A mantra in the group was: the degree of the truth of a man rested on the degree to which his actions matched his words. A corollary was: our true beliefs are not those handed to us, but the beliefs we actually live by… not just the ones that we carry because they sound like good ideas.

And now, I would like to introduce each man.

Adam

Relationships

Never being good enough. Doesn't matter how hard I try. There may be some short-term acceptance and positives but the overall thing is criticism. Not good enough and a withdrawal of love. I have a need to protect myself through anger and being closed. If I push them away they can't hurt me. But when I do so I feel such a sense of being alone and lonely and vulnerable and wanting the nurturing and acceptance and love. To me relationships are about the sharing of experiences and the lovely experience of being included in another's life. After this dance and a coming back together I am the one who cries and is the child. Why doesn't she ever let me be the one she cries with? Does she cry? Why can't I fulfill her needs? Why doesn't she let me in?

Through the pain there has been growth and understanding of both my Self and others. Why does the bad stuff sour the good stuff rather than the good stuff sweeten the bad? There is so much good stuff. There is a real spiritual and emotional connection. Why throw it all away? Nobody ever said it would be easy. I didn't know it would be this hard. Not being in a relationship simplifies so much. Being in a relationship complicates so much.

Why do I lose everything? (You can put the emphasis on each word in this question to come up with 5 questions). There is the pain of leaving every time I see them. Why give up now? Yes, there are plenty of reasons to separate, but I don't want to. There are reasons to stay together, as in the song, 'Love, Love Will Keep Us Together'.

Above all else there is a sense of belonging together. I don't want the pain. But I seem to get pain either way.

Criticism, Sarcasm, Blame and Accusation

When I receive criticism, blame, sarcasm or accusation from someone that has some sort of power over me (partner, parents, superiors at work) I almost immediately feel like a child. I feel weak, vulnerable, not good enough, failure. I get a feeling of powerlessness and impotence and I am unable to do or succeed. I get a feeling of unworthiness and that I should go away. I go in search of affirmation to pump myself back up.

If I don't think it's my fault I feel badly done by and tend to sulk. Then, after my initial reaction, or if I receive CBSA from someone who doesn't have 'power' over me, I lash out and attack through anger or sarcasm or justifying my position or belittling them.

Cycles, Seasons and Tides

I am in winter with the storms and tempest. It is dark thundery nights, lightning slashing the skies, rain beating down, coldness and harshness stinging my face. It is the winds buffeting me about with an immense power, massive chaos and destruction. Awesome. Beautiful. I always loved looking out the window at electrical storms lashing the trees, having the sense of being in a safe place as the spectator yet feeling the storm and being part of it and it me, seeking refuge from the storm yet being exhilarated by being caught in it: the fresh smell after rain; the cleansing. Looking forward to the spring.

The tide is washing out, taking good and bad with it. Hoping when it comes back in, some of the good is still there. Trusting that the storm will pass, that the spring will come, then summer. Knowing the tide will come back and, as always, will ebb; the essence of life;

and the certainty that all must occur. Making sure each time that we are better prepared. Making sure we enjoy the now... the positive aspects rather than fear what is certain to come.

Being thankful for what I've got. Letting go of what flows from my life. If it comes back in the next cycle good, if not, so be it.

Intimacy and Commitment

I find it hard to be with you because I'm scared of the separation (even though that's what I've got). I find it hard to enter into intimacy and commitment on an equal level. There always seems to be a power imbalance, a parent/child relationship, and a critical, punishing scenario. It happens in all aspects of our relationship: sex, work, money, sharing. Often I don't want to be punished so I put myself in the punisher's position. When I do this, softness will soften me. A connection will often snap me out of it. I so want to be an adult but find it so hard to maintain this state.

Rationing Love

I ration love by becoming needy so I can receive rather than give. The consequence of my actions is that I push people I love away if I do not have the reserves, so as not to be drained. I then feel so unloved and separate from them.

Looking Back

Dear Grandson,

When I am writing this your father is just a little boy (9 months old) with a smile that will light up the world. I'm very much looking forward to watching him grow and mature and become his own person. Your grandmother and I have just separated so I don't know how much I will have to do with your father or you. I'm scared that

I'm going to miss so much of your lives and I want you to have some sort of connection with how things are now.

We are in just the start of the 'Internet'. The world for me seems to be getting so much smaller but the distance between individuals seems to be getting farther apart. What we belong to often seems so big we don't feel we belong to anything. I hope you aren't experiencing the distance and loneliness this can bring.

I find solace in seeking community and sharing my life with a select number or group of people. There is a group I get together with called 'The Men's Group', probably one of the earlier organizations in the men's movement at the end of this century. I find the acceptance, forum of discovery and camaraderie a much valued and trusted part of my life. Remember my spirit runs through you, so trust that love and caring follow you and gain strength in the knowledge that you do belong.

Lots of love,
Your Grandfather
Adam

Fathers

I learned that to follow your moral value-base meant that you would be comfortable with your decisions but not always with the outcomes. I learned that family and community were important and that we should contribute of ourselves. I learned that we have choices in how we are in a situation. I wish he had taught me that I should focus more on myself, that I was as important as family and community.

That to subjugate my SELF for others all the time would lead to a draining of SELF. I wish he would have spent more time with me just letting me be, instead of always telling how I could or should improve or do better. I wish he had told me I was OK more often. I wish he had more of himself to give to me when he was around rather than spending himself on other kids or things so that when there was time for me he was tired or angry or critical or punishing me. I wish we could have been light and played, as I grew older, not just when I was a young child. I wish he hadn't shown how the faults/downfalls of others could disappoint so much. I wish he could have worked less and been lighter.

The Movement of Men

My search for meaning within my own self brought me to this men's group. It is a forum of discovery of who I am. Why I am the way I am. Why I do what I do. Why is my life the way it is? What is it in me that is controlling the way my life unfolds?

***The Men's Group** is a safe place in which to express what is in my heart, to receive nurturing and acceptance at a heart level from other men. It fills some of the holes in my experience as a male and enables me to grow through experiencing male in others. It is a celebration of being male and everything that goes with being a man. It nurtures the little boy and calms his fears. It revels in the power, joy, and uniqueness of us all. It honors the wisdom within us and helps us come up with some reasons and answers.*

My Eulogy

Adam was a man who was open to life.

He shared his love and wisdom unconditionally.

He always tried to make his life and the lives of those around him better.

He took to the task of life with all of the tools given him including his frailties and weaknesses.

He wasn't afraid to experience all of life's experiences.
He was gentle and kind.
He had an inner strength and an energy that seemed boundless.
He wasn't afraid to be seen as weak.
There was no façade.
Adam loved.

Brctt

Relationships

I am not sure that I know what the hardest thing for me to deal with is, so I'll just start writing. Maybe being not sure is part of it. Anyway, I do like to be thought of as intelligent, caring, in control, a leader and I do know that my wife thinks I am a klutz and insensitive and bullish at least at times. I have been with my wife for 20 years, off and on, and our relationship has spirit. So we have changed. I have changed.

Back to not sure. I have to think about that. I often feel vacuous, being the leader or sharing in leadership/direction-setting in our relationship. I need to break the cycle of external controls over my life. Some are good, like our children; some internal controls are not so good, like professional pride or some proposed idea of how to live, or fear of being vulnerable and not having cash-flow or financial security. I need to snap this cycle of direction-less activity. A lot of it does have direction/purpose/mutual agreement, but not all. And it's not a sense of wanting to dominate or have the power of the say

It's the sense of wanting to share and not knowing how. I have no intention of losing control. Trusting in my partner and the memories of both good and bad, of being "on the road. But life has to have passion. I need to reconcile the mundane elements, rather than being subsumed by them. I have a sense of not wanting to 'throw the baby out with the bath water'. Yet I probably need some change in my life and yet I am unsure of what or how. I want to share all this but I am afraid to. I do not trust enough.

Cycles, Seasons and Tides

Spring. My wife and I have planted seedlings; re-potted, laid the pea straw and the blossoms are going for it. I know that I need to keep working/fertilizing to pump up the buds and that if I don't pick up the things that I have worked on through the winter and the proceeding autumn then I won't have the fruit at the end of the summer that I would like. This I must keep at.

I feel urgency. I know many tasks that I must keep at and I know that it is best to do this with my wife, my children, friends and colleagues. I know I will have many regrets but I also know I will continue to thrive. I reflect because I have just come out of winter when it was bleak and when a moment seemed to last forever and it was cold and bare.

Intimacy and Commitment

The intimacy/commitment/closeness to my wife is the most important thing in my life and I sure as hell don't have the answers and there are a few obstacles.

I have had twenty years of partnership, with early intimacy, times of oneness and years of mistrust. One thousand times accused of poor communication or none, which was mostly right. Commitment has meant career, children, debts, social responsibilities, etc. My wife wants more. Night after night we can sit in front of the TV. She has got about as much good conversation as I have. I am bitter. Seems there is just more drawing from the well. It is good to talk, when we do. I get so caught up in things outside our relationship that are important and I expect her to support me.

Looking Back

Dear Grandson,

I trust that I relay a message of optimism and that you, too, can share an optimistic/positive view of the world. Many might say I am a fool but maybe I'm a romantic fool. Your grandmother and I continue to grow together, albeit painfully. I wish she could make more rational discussions and put into place the building blocks for change; she wants me to be ruled by the heart and passionate like I was when we first met. Regardless, we love one another deeply and will continue to shape and modify our lives with the pushes and pulls of these different innate perspectives. We have only one another to hug and we know our shared loneliness, our mortality and our desire for intimacy. How could you not be optimistic? (Is the world less scary? Less tough for you? Have people stopped killing one another en masse yet, etc.).

Pass my love onto your father and mother. I hope they taught you better than I taught them (or for that matter my father taught me). I am at a men's group at the time of writing, talking about men's needs to express emotion and support one another and sharing with other men. I believe that this will better help me to understand my relationship with your grandmother and my children. Time will tell. I know my own father had no such luxuries. Take care.

All my love,
Your Grandfather

Fathers

Did learn not to judge others, stoically grin and bear it, hard work (physical and mental) pays off, constancy, the subtlety of conveying affection, to be tough, to be cynical, to beware, to be stable. I learnt from my father that life can be cruel and hard and that talk is cheap. I learnt that compromise should not be entered into easily and that privacy (a man's home is his castle) is the peak experience. I would have liked to learn more about kindness in the family, about warmth and caring. I would also have liked to learn more about how to deal with pent-up anger effectively. Family pride he taught me but it wasn't always something to be proud of. Perseverance (of an ill) is not always a good thing.

Did not have him take me to my footy matches as a junior. When he did turn up it was like he was being critical. I did not learn how to take criticism well from my father. I doubt that I handle criticism of my son all that well. I would have liked praise when it was due.

The Movement of Men

I came to the group because a male friend was going and he asked me to come too. I had a range of serious matters, mostly with my wife that I wanted to take 'time out' over, to think about and so learn from other men or share with them. I had little fear of this process as I am prepared to confront myself/my life/my feelings. Not all is perfect. I came for help and I got it.

I found the men in the group all dealing with issues in their lives and having the courage to acknowledge them and wanting to do something about it/grow. All this was normal everyday/everybody/everyman stuff. I get out of this process a sense of belonging without fierce competition and of each other trying to contribute to their own and other's development. This sounds insane but it is not. True. It is simple.

My Eulogy

Brett was a man who was generous in all ways.

He could be relied upon to be there when needed and to listen and help without judging or asking for reasons or rhymes.

He could be tough but this was not what mattered most for his toughness came from genuine concern and the need for someone to step forward when things were off the rails.

The breadth of his shoulders matched the depth of his heart for it was passion that drove him.

His relationship with those closest did not sit stagnant but was vibrant and alive.

We will all miss him, many of us loved him well and those closest knew of his honesty and willingness to confront.

In death he both departs and returns.

Carl

Relationships

Now that I understand that women think and process differently to men I can accept criticism more readily than I could earlier in my relationship. The next hardest thing that I have had to deal with is rejection. Not only in my relationship with my wife but rejection by others throughout my whole life.

Apart from the programmed rejection by my mother over the years I have hurtful memories of the rejection by my first girlfriend when I was eleven. This was only a sample of things to come. Afterwards I would deliberately not become involved for fear of being hurt again. That was until I fell in love and got married when I was 25. (Although I can remember at the time almost having two voices one saying how great it was to be in love and the other saying that I should get the hell out of here because you're going to get hurt again). At least the first time was quick. The last one has gone on for nearly 20 years although there are signs that improvement is happening. Even then, rejection, even if it only lasts for a couple of days, is extremely hard to deal with as a man. Today I handle rejection differently. I realize I am the only one who can reject me.

Cycles, Seasons and Tides

I feel that I am in the spring of my life after having experienced a rebirth. By rebirth I mean I have been lucky enough to be able to take stock of my life so far by sitting back and quickly letting it all flow before me, from birth, through childhood to teenage years, early adulthood, marriage, children, careers, etc. In sitting outside my own story it all becomes so much clearer to me.

My springtime means that I am on a journey of discovery, of growth, of leaving behind the conditioned man that I had become and embarking on the man I wanted to be as a young child, a loving, caring, creative boy who has physically matured and spiritually developed. I am happy with myself and in hope of spreading that philosophy by being an example for others to follow, particularly other men. I am happy in my lofty nest and will be even happier when those in the valley are the same.

Intimacy and Commitment

Intimacy for me is fearful because of the opposite side to it – rejection. What goes around comes around: therefore, no intimacy, less likelihood of rejection. I have found that the smaller amount of intimacy, the softer the rejection. Intimacy is closest when experienced during sex.

Intimacy is losing masculinity. It is even instinctual as if this was the way it has always been. I love intimacy but am fearful of it.

The greatest intimate experience I had was being washed and bathed and massaged by seven women at the same time whilst doing group work in Bali. It was a total surrender on my part. There was no need to speak after it. My body said it all.

Looking Back

I am living in the city of Melbourne in a suburb to the northeast of the city. I work for a large organization. I am married and have three boys and one girl, all of whom are at school, at university, secondary college or primary school. We live on an acre in a large house by today's standards so it gives us all plenty of space to move round in or to get lost in when we need to do so.

My wife works four days per week as well to provide our family with the standard of living we would like to share with them. Whilst it places a bit of strain on our marriage relationship it is what we both desire to make our children's opportunities to be as good as we were both given by our parents. They actually achieved the same goal albeit on lesser incomes and lower social status. It makes one question the process but when we see the rapid development of mankind intellectually we can see the advantages. However, there also comes with it some disadvantages, for people tend to forget about what is needed for a balance in life.

There is a movement amongst the intelligentsia that perhaps we have become too focused on developing the intellect and now is a time to start balancing our lives with both left and right side brain activity. We have seen the damage caused by the massive and destructive wars of the 20th century. Whilst little 'wars' have occurred it is evident that there is a growing push for peace amongst all nations. This excites me greatly. I have many fears about the future for my grandchildren and their children in terms of the environmental damage that progress has caused. I fear that the beauty in nature, the forests and the clean free-flowing rivers may not be there to be enjoyed by the generations to follow. This also concerns me greatly but I need to be more active in seeing to it that some of the damage is stopped before it is too late.

Fathers

I learnt how not to do it by living the experience of my relationship with my father. I have been able to have the relationship with my sons that I did not have with my father. There have been lessons that I did not learn at times. I repeated the cycle sometimes and this seemed to be more with my eldest son when he became a teenager. I suppose I was always a positive sort of person. My father was extremely negative and I have seen the damage that he has caused amongst my brothers and sisters. My eldest son tends to be negative at times and I find that difficult to cope with because it is my father and I all over but in reverse roles.

Sometimes I lack a lot of confidence and whilst on the surface I appear to others as being in total control, I am actually proving to my father that I am good enough but always fearful of failure. Through the men's group I was able to learn how to address a lot of these issues with my father before he died. I wished he had been more open and intimate with me. And I wish he had been more reassuring rather than the constant negatives that actually spurred me on.

I wished that he would actually touch or hug me. He finally did when he was over 70 years of age. I am not missing that opportunity with my own sons.

The Movement of Men

Curiosity brought me to ***The Men's Group*** *that I heard about after going through marriage guidance counseling. At first, I thought it was a bit strange mainly because it was the antithesis of my conditioning as a man. Here were men being open with other men, talking about their own fears, etc. and their fears for the world at large. The group has a core that continues to use the group to keep in touch with their own feminine qualities and are pretty genuine. Some pass through when the novelty wears off and these people either pursue spiritual growth elsewhere or stop their own development.*

The men's group is a place to learn about meditation, relaxation, coping with being male, how to improve our interrelationship with females, how to lead by example and try to change society itself.

Change is, of course, for the better. A more caring, gentler, softer man will eventually spread so that mankind can live in peace.

I enhance my spiritual growth from attending the men's group and I learn to drop the masks and to become who I really am and don't bother about what others think. The men's group is my time for me.

My Eulogy

Carl was a happy person who seemed to become softer and more open as he aged.

Early in his life he was always in a hurry to achieve things be it on the sporting arena or in his career as an accountant.

He appeared lost for most of his life despite being married and having four beautiful children.

It was not until his mother died that he really started to look at himself and the hatred he held for his father, who had mistreated him as a young child up to the time he left home at age 19.

In later years Carl became a very talented artist and was able to retire from his profession and be creative.

He also had a great love of thoroughbreds and actually had a horse that was quite successful in Melbourne racing circles. He would often say that the horse was an extension of himself, a free spirit.

Carl lived until a ripe old age and helped many young people find their paths in this journey we call life.

Darren

Relationships

What hurts the most in looking back at relationships is that they can be so painful, with the loss of opportunity or how it could have been better, and in not being trusted enough to be told something, to be spoken to honestly.

That's exactly what I did with one woman. I had angst I couldn't express, couldn't utter. A façade of normality and 'happy families' resulted with lava boiling underneath. The more we pretended things were fine, the harder it became to explore or release what was going on underneath.

My mum is a shell, and we rarely see much of what's inside. She tells stories of her adventures when she was young and would subtly have a go at Dad for not being sporty or glamorous. She very rarely speaks of him with love, just respect and a bit of duty. Her 'breakdown', (illness and addiction), brought her to the edge of opening up, but the sense of loss and risk was too great and she retreated back into her happy family/duty/martyrdom shell. I rarely speak to her honestly and try to protect her from anything remotely connected with criticism by going to safe areas.

Criticism from Mum was devastating, infrequent and always given with an excuse so I didn't lose face. I was never smacked but can remember almost every (infrequent) word of reproach. It was always glowing praise for me.

We don't know each other very well! The loss when she dies, if things are the same as now, is that 32-year-old me never saw the

32-year-old her. I never knew what she felt or thought other than duty, with a bit of bitterness slipped in as a guilt trip.

Perhaps rejection is encased in that refusal to allow me or us in to her real feelings because they're too bad to express. I feel sorry for her and feel guilt and sadness about her life sitting in front of the TV while Dad was out seemingly rejecting her. Could I say that to Dad? I have Mum's fear that it would be so hurtful, never forgotten, always over our interactions like a dark cloud, that's why we never say anything! It's unthinkable to express anger because all words will be remembered, judged by a rational listening ear; in our family, logic is greater than emotion; emotion can be dismantled to nothing because of its lack of logic. My well of anger <u>needs</u> either contact sport or an abrupt word from someone, in a bad mood to light my fuse and allow me to express some emotion.

My first romantic relationships were almost non-existent. I always wanted to be included. I wouldn't settle for anything/anyone ordinary. I had impossibly high targets that I never achieved. I was never constant enough with anyone to give it a chance. I meet them later and we actually like each other! Such a need pervaded these interactions. I miss those people; I wanted to be loved by them; I feel I could never contact them because my lingering need to be loved would betray my wife or because they'd be married and their husbands would wonder, 'What's this guy doing ringing you up?' I feel so much loss, so many regrets and have so many 'if onlys', so much idolizing and fantasizing and not being present.

Several of these relationships remain tinted with regret. I want to re-live these, to really be there and have another feeling from them rather than loss. Without peace with these women, I don't feel fully here in my marriage, and yet, I hate separation and holding back. I don't feel I could talk about this angst with my wife!

Cycles, Seasons and Tides

The summer arrives, but with all the ripening and with all its rewards comes the hint that it won't last. It never lasts. The leaves are falling and things always come back down to earth. What a cruel juxtaposition that once things seem really good and when I am on a high, it simply means that there is further to fall. 'This too shall pass' are the wise words for all occasions.

The balance comes from seeing all things in cycles and eventually experiencing them all. With the rewards from one part of life come the reminders of grief. With the disappointments comes knowledge that surprises are sure to spring up from the earth. Perhaps to live in all seasons and see their balance is to be ethereal; instead I am a rock, which endures them all rather than rejoicing in them. I pride myself on my tough, hard, unflinching nature. I hold myself back from having fun. I am heavy because I do not trust that I will come up again with the bubbles but rather stay stuck down in the mud

I am addicted to late autumn and winter through their heaviness. I know I'm alive; I don't let myself have much spring and summer. And as for the tides: I had so much fun on holiday a few weeks ago, allowing myself to be washed in and out and pushed around by small waves breaking on the sand. I rarely go with the flow with such abandon and trust. I look for an anchor, an insurance policy, so that the guilt and disappointment are never too bad; thus, even my fun is planned and controlled, and I have little exhilaration, excitement and passion. If I can say "Shit, this is bad" and stay with it and accept I have made a loss, I suspect I shall be freer to say 'Shit, this is good!'

Intimacy and Commitment

I feel safer with men. Men understand. Once after a break-up where I felt trapped I finally left. My female friends, my sisters and my mother were aghast, and thought I was an absolute beast. All took the same side (of the oppressed woman) and intimated that I had no right to feel as I felt. But at the football club: men with whom I'd almost never expressed anything personal with all knew the feeling. All accepted me (whether or not they knew or approved of various details).

With commitment, the fear is what if I say yes to this and something better comes along? I couldn't say that to a woman. They'd be shocked, suspect me of thinking it all the time (even if I am!). Commitment is loss of the opportunity to scale mountains, boldly venture on adventures. Commitment to me is knowing I can't change my mind, have sex with someone younger, firmer or sexier, EVER.

If I am intimate and reveal these feelings to a woman, especially the ones who come up again and again, I am being threatening or hurtful. There is no gain in expressing something I feel would be held against me and never understood. Sometimes I look at women in terms of bloodlines or in terms of 'wouldn't it be easier if I went for someone simpler. Are there women who really love sex?'

Looking Back

Dear Darren,

Firstly may I say how proud I was when you were named Darren and how glad I am that you have finally found this letter? I wonder if you can imagine that I am in the prime of my life, six foot one inch, that's 185 cm, and about 80 kg. I have had two knee operations and have given away contact sport, but I am still a pretty fit bloke.

I wonder what my father was up to when he was my age. My sister was one year old, and my mother would have been just pregnant with my brother.

Anyway, now my work is full of promise. I have just passed my exam to begin specialist training and am quite highly regarded by my peers. But I love being the odd one out. I meditate, I love football and I have a ponytail. All quite strange for a professional. I think that hits upon why I have the regard of my peers. I am much more open to the emotional side of where I work and experience than most. My greatest achievements have been befriending clients and communicating with them and their families at a deep level. This is the part of my work that I aspire to. I wonder what will have happened when this letter is read.

Australia is a great place to live. My wife and I really love being close to nature. In times when we did not live close to our families we paid the price of only seeing them a few days every year. I missed the closeness of being around family and friends I have known for a long time. Having people I can confide in and who support me is something I really treasure.

As I write this I am looking forward to coming back home to Melbourne. As a young man I feel young when I talk to some people and old when I talk to others. Despite my steps towards professionalism, part of me would trade it all to be good enough to take a big mark at the MCG on Grand Final day; I'd really love to add my professional skills to a football club, but a couple of years ago it didn't feel important enough to settle for that. I hope I'll go back to it.

I fear the future to some degree, and have all sorts of insurance policies to try to assuage the fear! I fear being lonely one day, although I suspect I never will; I fear being busy and not around to play with my kids. I want to teach my kids how to kick a footy and so on. I fear my parents' deaths, and hope that I'm open enough with my wife and kids that when I die, they'll be sad, but not too frustrated.

Good luck to you!

With all my love,

Darren xxxx

Fathers

I am so scared that you'll die. I wish you'd have been around more to play with me, to help me, to kick a footy more than the two times I can remember, to play cricket more than the once or twice. To teach me how to hold a cricket bat, even though you didn't know.

You did know camping. Why didn't we go camping more? Why did you leave Mum in front of the TV so often for so many years? You withdrew. If you die soon, you'll leave our family with a feeling of repressed emotion. I wish I knew you well enough to be angry with you sometimes. I got from you an enormous capacity to love at a community and platonic level but a difficulty expressing it on a person-to-person level. We needed a special occasion to feel it. Such moments were great, but love was very rarely expressed for the hell of it.

I got your hands and feet. I love them. I got your love of nature, plants, country, and the wild. I got your deep sadness when your mum died, when you took that phone call in the front hall when I was about seven. How hard was it, knowing that we hated her?

I got your sense of being busy doing things that can't be criticized. I got your love, but your strangled inability to show it easily. I got your wisdom. I hope you don't die for a long time.

With all my love,

Darren xxx

The Movement of Men

I am so tired of having to be strong and responsible. I am weighed down by the pressure of providing for my family for the rest of our lives. I am sick of having to be patient and reasonable every minute of the day.

I am sick of competing with every other man in the world. Am I younger? Stronger? Tougher? Smarter? Do I earn more? Is my dick bigger?

I am so frustrated with sex; I mourn and yearn for the uncommitted part of me that attracted admiring glances from women and could act upon them. I hate feeling trapped in a relationship and not being able to speak of it, to feel guilty for even thinking it, or fantasizing about other women. I am scared about the future. I am so angry, tired and fed up. None of this stuff could I say before I started doing personal growth work, and no matter how much work my wife and I do, it's still so much easier in a group of men.

It is such a relief to let my guard down. It is so amazing and supportive to hear my fears and frustrations voiced by others, as if we speak. At times it is as if we speak from one collective angst. It is so good to trust. We have such a hard shell that is such a joy when mine is cracked and those of other men. And it's great that there are women's groups for the women, men's groups for us, and everything else for when we feel safe and strong enough to test the water!

My Eulogy

There are tears, but the eyes that cry them glisten.

No floods of grief, because most completion was done in life.

Darren was lots of fun, and very loving, and once he finally accepted and loved himself and let us all in, we loved being around him.

He loved gardens and flowers, and would like to think that seeds were planted in his name, and that he was remembered in their beauty, their blossoms and their fruit.

He loved living, and he loved joking.

If it's possible to visit from the spirit world or wherever that part of him has gone, he'll be back. But rather than a creaking floorboard in a hallway at night, he'll probably be the one who moved your keys so you can't find them.

Darren would this last time like to honor his wife, his family and all his other teachers, and trusts that their love and beauty will continue to inspire others.

Darren sends blessings and peace to us all.

Eric

Relationships

My commitment/allegiance to a relationship is my greatest fear. I don't ever have a long-term relationship with anyone who constantly criticizes. The relationship rapidly changes if the criticism is not warranted. I'm handling rejection OK. I've had so much over the years. But this will probably be tested again in the future when I 'love' someone again.

My lack of commitment to a relationship is reflected in the type of relationship. I'm committed to my two youngest children. They come first over all other things. My eldest daughter is going her way and my commitment to her is to 'be there' when wanted.

My two long-term relationships with girlfriends over the past five years have been on my terms only and I guess the commitment reflects how much I'm in the relationship. Don't know whether I'm so selfish but I don't wish to expend too much energy in developing relationships.

Cycles, Seasons and Tides

Winter is the season where I am: (1) awaiting the next growth spurt; (2) alone on a personal/intimate level (my contact with others is as desired); (3) in the middle of winter, or approaching spring but not cold; and (4) I'm quite warm inside and out but there is a temperature that reminds me of winter. All this keeps me looking after and caring for myself.

In terms of the tide, I'm on the incoming tide, just after the wave, because: (1) it is starting to happen; (2) nourishment and support is abundant; (3) the waves are 'fuller' and not dumping on the sand as hard. The water is less murky; and (4) it is not full moon, so not expecting flood tides.

Intimacy and Commitment

I have been "savaged" financially in divorce. Why should I risk intimacy again? I can get sex/pleasures/dominant feeling/thrills more often than ever before at the present time. I fear intimacy in long-term relationships. In a casual relationship I speak my mind and my beliefs. Maybe I am frightened they'll be used against me in the future in a long-term relationship. I'm selfish. By being intimate or committing, I feel I'm going to hurt the person more when it breaks up.

Looking Back

I get excited by: (1) money was relatively easy to come by and this enabled varied holidays, (scuba diving, skiing, overseas trips); possessions were plentiful and we didn't want for much; (2) women had equal billing with men, which made for easier living in most ways. I mean I didn't have to supply entertainment for women, as they were often able to go and get it themselves; and (3) technology is exploding.

What I found was that money was more important than truth to most people. That family life was disposable and people moved freely away with a minimum of effort. Computerization seems to destroy the art of communication. Well-being came to me by closing the door and being by myself whenever I wished. True friendships enabled me to change my business conditions for my later working life.

These are mixed years as I found myself having to regroup financially from ground zero. But they have been good years as I have spent valuable time with my children as they developed into adults.

Fathers

The positive learning was not being afraid of hard work, honesty and trust. Family education is important. Don't live beyond your means. Show respect for other people. When you do a job do it to the best of your ability. He was very proud of me and other siblings. He allowed freedoms that in retrospect were generous. Even though he worked late hours, he usually was always there.

Negative learning was a poor ability regarding business, poor control of temper and expression of feelings.

I would like to have received: (1) a clear example of making sure you look after yourself and love yourself uppermost, and (2) an example of good family communication as he was the figurehead of the family.

The Movement of Men

*A breakdown in a marriage brought me to **The Men's Group**. It's an opportunity to further life's journey by starting the best journey of inward reflection. It is an atmosphere where it is soon discovered that my problems are not new to me but occur to everyone in varying ways. So what one expresses is felt by all! It is a caring group that gives support, understanding and love.*

It is not the most important part of my life. I meet once a month where I can re-acquaint myself with those aspects of male being that may not be able to be experienced in the workplace/leisure time. I get a wonderful opportunity to have professional psychology guidance (at low cost) to give me the chance to know myself and thus take actions to enable me to get where I want, both in work and relationships.

My Eulogy

Eric was a person who experienced and lived life to the fullest.

In his living he had three facets: his family life, his business life and his personal life.

In his personal life, he was at peace with himself from the age of forty-eight.

He acknowledged the vigor and turmoil of life and just accepted them and moved on.

He was a wonderful benefactor giving to those charities he had interest in, in proportions that are wonderful to see.

Family life was so important and he enjoyed watching his children grow and make similar mistakes that he made.

Eric was always there for consultation and help if asked for.

He acknowledges his first wife was a good mother who managed to put into their lives the opportunity to see other ways besides those of their mother.

Professional life saw him dedicated and working long hours till the age of forty-eight when he managed to reduce that load and enjoy fully all that he did. This was reflected in the care and success of his investments.

He has done with his money and life all that he wished to do.

Eric, we have enjoyed your life with us and will remember you for your actions and love.

Francis

Relationships

Relationships to me bring the fear of loss, abandonment and rejection. It's the rejection that triggers the fear of loss and abandonment.

The difficulty of not losing myself in the relationship, being able to be in a relationship and still be me. This used to be difficult for me; however, it is not so difficult in my current relationship (my marriage) where we still both have a clear identity. There is mutual respect.

My early childhood relationships, especially with my parents, amazingly had the themes of abandonment (both emotional and physical). My early relationships were also more co-dependent in their nature and looking back were not healthy. It was not until my mid-twenties that I entered what I believe to be good relationship. Being with someone because I wanted to be, not because I needed to be.

It is hard for me to be in a relationship and not lose my identity and my sense of who I am. The fears of loss and abandonment still live in my psyche though and events can still trigger those early childhood feelings. Hearing another man's feelings of loss and abandonment today and listening to his hurt bring these feelings up in me. Loss and abandonment are things I can easily identify with.

Cycles, Seasons and Tides

I am now going into spring. I thought I had been in spring, but it was really a deep, cold, blistering dark winter. Only the realization of this enabled me to enter spring and I am connecting again with

Self. I am now better able to connect with my partner and baby son. I have a realization that today's events still trigger feelings from the past. I have to be in touch with it as my adult self, and not hide from it by distancing, withdrawing, over-reacting. I realize that after all the years at university I am doing something I don't want to do.

But I can do what I want. It takes action, more study and effort. So I am in spring, a re-growth. However, to get here, I had to go into the dark depths of winter.

Intimacy and Commitment

When I am connected with my 'Self', I can be intimate, give myself fully and 'be there' with the person I am with. Occasionally, I am not connected with my true Self and feel the need to push away or disconnect. Sometimes I even feel engulfed. During these times, intimacy is very difficult and sometimes feels impossible. It is a time when I really need to be on my own, to connect with myself again.

Another fear that comes with intimacy is letting down my barriers and fully exposing myself. Maybe this is to do with the fear of rejection or abandonment?

Looking Back

I am writing this at a time of great change. The relationships between men and women have changed, with traditional female tasks now being increasingly shared by men. There was greater awareness of the difficulties in being 'male' and 'female' among the sexes. Living life was exciting, a time of change and new opportunities. There were also fears, such as a growing fear of personal safety and a need to be aware of it, as well as fears of loss.

There was a need to be flexible in work and there was a great change in the nature of work. There was a greater need to understand people. People began not to just work to live, but to look for greater meaning and intrinsic value in what they did. They began to 'enjoy work'. There were also increasing opportunities to become distracted, to lose the real sense of what life was about, what we wanted. Apart from the ways of creating excitement out there, excitement also came from discovering other things about my Self and finding a greater understanding and peace.

These years were a time for growth for me, and the greatest years of my life. I have learnt more about work and myself. Your grandmother and I lived life to the full. Your father was born and I finally found peace within myself.

Fathers

The negatives and positives were I learnt to be responsible, not to trust, how to be anxious, a strong work ethic, a sense of resilience. That whatever life hands us, we can get through it.

I needed him: to be there in my childhood to have saved me from my mother and to have displayed his love; to have told me he was proud of me when I was younger, not to have waited until I was in my late twenties; unconditional acceptance; to have spent more time with me when I was growing up; to have bought me a present instead of always giving me a check; to have told me I'm good enough; to have given me some 'valuable time'; and to have allowed a relationship to grow in my early years when I really needed him, not until I was 18+.

The Movement of Men

An 'inner void' brought me to ***The Men's Group****. It was a need to better understand my experience as a man. Do any other men share my feelings? Do any other men have similar difficulties/experiences to me in their lives? A men's group is a safe, accepting environment for men to speak and be heard without criticism or judgment. It is a way of giving and sharing yourself with other men.*

It is also a place for healing and 're-fathering'. It fills that inner yearning I have had, to have my life and experiences validated by other men. I also learn by listening to other men's experiences. ***The Men's Group*** *is a reflection of myself.*

My Eulogy

Francis was a bright, happy child like many children begin in life, until around the age of five when his parents divorced and the family home was sold.

He had a difficult childhood, an unhappy one.

His mother was never really there emotionally for him and his father did not take a very active interest in his life in his early years.

He was an unhappy, lost, disconnected little boy.

He overcame this, got out of his unhappy situation and began to develop his sense of self.

He was no longer held back.

He went to university, graduated and began a successful career in which he rose to senior positions by his mid-twenties. People who worked with him described him as a dynamic, assertive individual.

His early relationships with women were not good, usually being attracted to the wrong type of person.

Francis continued to work on himself in his twenties, spent time alone and healed many childhood wounds that many of us carry around forever.

During this time alone, when he was not looking for a relationship, he met the woman he would share his life with until his death; and he began a positive, healthy relationship with a strong, loving woman who understood him.

They truly shared their lives together in a relationship that most described as full of mutual respect, honesty and love.

By his thirties, he was no longer fulfilled with his work and undertook further study that enabled him to make a complete career change.

This allowed him to do what he really loved and found real meaning in until his death.

Francis was a good husband and father, always available to his wife and children, who he encouraged to grow as he continually did.

He loved life and lived it to the full, always continually working on keeping connected to his true 'Self', which so many of us disconnect with during our lives.

He was an achiever, and those who knew him found him loving, honest and caring.

Greg

Relationships

The role that I am portrayed to play can be one of the hardest things to deal with in a relationship. There is no clear pathway for me. I see myself as the provider, the comforter, and the strength. The expectations are there that comes with a sense of fear: can I be all these things successfully? If not, where will it lead? To rejection and cynicism?

The other thing that is hard in a relationship is the facing up to my own weaknesses that are seen by my partner, and how I react or act with those actions.

Sharing is also one of the hardest things to deal with, especially the sharing of my inner thoughts and feelings. In my case, being an only child, I have very much kept my thoughts and feelings to myself. It's not an easy transition to make, to change from a life of self-consultations. Not showing caring or love is also difficult for me.

Cycles, Seasons, and Tides

I'm in a Melbourne winter/spring. One minute the sun shines. Life is great; the next is snow and rain. The next there are flowers and the trees have blossomed. There is little consistency both in my emotional and physical feeling as I come to grips with myself and grapple with how I feel and how others make me feel.

Once I was very clear on what my goals were and what I wanted to be. However I am now not so clear. I have changed in what I want and where I want to be in 10, 20, 30 years.

Intimacy and Commitment

Total and absolute commitment can be extremely scary. There is a fear of giving everything and someone else having such a large part of me; my fears, pleasures and hopes. How will the other person use this incredible information? How will my partner react to all my feelings? Will it coincide with hers?

Total commitment means total disclosure of myself. I feel that this can leave me exposed to pain. I feel that it could be used against me, and would cause irreparable damage to my relationship.

Looking Back

As I write this I am in a period of development for me. I made the transition from a youth to an adult. I got married and started a house and family. Every moment there have been new discoveries both in myself as a person as well as in my skills and demands upon myself. My most exciting time was my meeting and marrying your grandmother.

There are also fears on how the future will turn out. How I can achieve my responsibilities. I had a great feeling of success when I finished my degree and proved to myself that I could achieve as much as I wanted.

It is a time I am learning to believe in myself. In a sense I had to believe in my Self. Sharing the 90s with someone who truly cares for me and helps to teach me how to share gives me a great feeling of satisfaction and well-being.

The 90s are a time of changing roles for men: a time when new values, new experiences are being formed and men have started to lose what was once the norm. Thus it is a time of positive turbulence and growth for men and women.

Fathers

I learnt how I would not like to treat my children or my wife. I also learnt that staying together matters, loyalty.

I would have loved to have received love, sharing and some positive feedback and reinforcement, rather than negative. I would have loved to be able to talk to him as an equal and enjoy his thoughts or his feelings for his family and sharing my feelings with him.

The Movement of Men

***The Men's Group** gives me the opportunity to see what other men experience and feel. It allows me a forum to view my life and question what is happening, question my actions and reactions to situations. It allows me to process my experiences now and how they were affected by past experience. It allows me to share my experiences with others and how they have handled situations.*

It is truly a learning experience, which allows me to feel things: emotions, anger, pain, sadness, and happiness in which I just wouldn't make the time for in any other time.

My Eulogy

Greg was fortunate to have experienced many and varying cultures, lifestyles and people.

He was one that believed that everyone had some good in them.

He saw the positive aspect in all things.

He believed that men of all races could live together in peace.

He was a loving husband and trusted friend, who would be there in crises or need.

He was a person of courage and full of life and joy and loved being amongst people.

He loved challenging his own thoughts and ideas as well as those of others.

Howard

Relationships

Without the other there is no relationship. Relationships become stuffed up when the other or I lose our Selves in our 'stuff'.

The hardest things that I have to deal with in relationships are the times when I am not connected with my spiritual side. When this happens I have an absence of self, of self-trust and an ability to communicate the appropriate and authentic message to the other. The message is always the emotional source of my vulnerability and inability to connect with myself.

The self-separation occurs when I am tired, lonely, worried, being criticized or perceive criticism from others. It happens when there are unspoken, unclarified or unacknowledged issues and expectations in others or myself. It also exists when I want attention or feel unsafe or threatened.

All the above have their genesis in my early childhood and teenage years. Abandoned in a boarding school at seven years old, criticism and abuse by a neurotic, manipulative, selfish but loving mother, humiliation in school because of a late developing body are all contributing causes to subconscious mechanisms of self-separation.

Since acknowledging the emotions of my past pains, labeling and communicating them to a partner, my relationship improves with every day. Such activity has allowed for compassion and love to grow for each other.

Criticism, Blame, Sarcasm and Accusation

Criticism, blame, sarcasm and accusation all affect me similarly. If I feel there is an element of truth then I am less than perfect

Cycles, Seasons and Tides

My life has four elements: spiritual, physical, emotional and intellectual. As my growth continues as a man this time around I travel to the center of my existence and learn the middle path: sometimes in pain, at others in joy. I know these flow together as a tune or song line; a high now will surely change to a low tomorrow and vice versa. I struggle for equanimity and self-acceptance in each and all.

So where am I in my seasons? I am in late spring for spirituality. An awakening has occurred and a model now exists that I follow and that I understand. Surrendering to this path is my challenge. The center or homecoming will be joy, love and connectedness.

Physical aspects of my life have been in dormant winter for many years. I now perceive these fallow years to have been self-imposed. Escape from the chills of winter is to just do things: walk, diet, cycle, make love, all with enjoyment and abandonment to the activity itself and not to fear or be held back by the concept of failing.

Emotional aspects are again in spring bloom; feeling, smelling, touching, seeing, tasting my life are sensed at a high previously held suppressed because of the expectations of others in not showing tears and shouts. Fears, rejection and anger are now being released and mixed with those of joy and laughter of the Cosmic Joke.

Intellectual aspects are in the full growth of summer. All seeds now bear the fruit of the hard work, persistence, experience and knowledge. Complacency, arrogance and intellectual control are my potential nemesis. Developing humility and teaching my truth to others is my salvation.

Intimacy and Commitment

It is courageous indeed to tell women in practical ways of how I am crippled in intimacy and risk hurting them or experiencing their rejection. Up until recently, I have tried to communicate this difficulty to women, although it is only recently that I have become aware that it was this fear of intimacy and commitment that prevented relationships from consolidating.

My fear was born from early childhood days and then a twenty-year marriage where rejection and abandonment occurred. I now take responsibility for these deficits in myself and for communicating them.

Life on both sides of the gender barrier is less than a perfect process. I am learning that by eliminating the barrier I am dealing more compassionately with others. I want to catch and stop unspoken expectations. I want to know myself first and love myself deeply, even before I come together with another so that I can also be accepting and nurturing of the other.

I had a real and frightening experience in my early days. It was my mother who I even now love and honor with an impatient and unspoken kindly anger. Paradoxes yet and perhaps ever unresolved.

As I grow, doubts will arise when I lose contact with myself. Then I need to be honest. I know that without another I am in an unfulfilled life. Love and growth are painful if I trap another into my selfish needs.

Looking Back

I think that the Western materialistic way of life that had developed so rapidly after the Second World War had turned sour for individuals, families, communities, nations and the world. The technological age had failed to deliver what was promised or naively assumed.

Pollution of the planet and destruction of the environment was obvious. Family and community structures were breaking down. People were made redundant.

Your family and I were both an active and passive part of that degradation and suffered in all facets of our lives. Even so as I was coming into maturity I inherited the responsibility for solving some of these issues. Fortunately, a movement commencing during my youth took bloom. New teachers emerged, communities commenced to re-establish themselves that cared for each other, themselves and the planet. Businesses knew they had to relearn and go on learning if they were to survive the rapid changes. They had to find new ways that didn't rely on material growth but a personal growth and mastery. We began to see tangible evidence of a new dawn for civilization.

Work was a means of survival, an essential part of my conscious life. It is the intellectual and physical effort required to provide an interest, money and lifestyle. Work both invigorated and tired me. It rejuvenated and aged me. Work created tension with other areas of my life particularly the spiritual and emotional aspects. I got enjoyment, excitement, and financial and spiritual rewards. Maturity and growth came in steps as I learned to understand the motives of others and myself.

There was an urgent and critical race for society. The previous poor and underdeveloped nations wanted equivalent wealth that the Western World had established. The challenges that arose were how to share the existing wealth of the world with the other without suffering hardship ourselves. The challenge excited me. My time had come. I survived and grew by following a path of personal development and growth that eventually I had to take to teach to others.

Fathers

My father taught me that he loved me as a child. He demonstrated loyalty, perseverance in work and pain, diplomacy, tact, dry humor, honor and an appreciation of tolerance for the other person regardless of their point of view. He gave me a sense of presence, standing and personal respect for others that emerged in latter years. Dad taught me to honor and respect women even in their most strident and vindictive state of being.

He did not teach or give me self-esteem or that I was worthy even just being me. He did not teach me how to physically love a woman or how to effectively communicate with her or how to be intimate with her.

I would have loved to have been his friend and known him as a man.

The Movement of Men

Having completed a twenty-year marriage with its failure, redundancy at work, a son in hospital with extensive burns and subsequently living away from home, I undertook persona-development courses to determine what part I had contributed to this Samsara of life. At no time did I want or work for anything but the best for my family and employers. I believe I loved them all the time.

I learnt that in this trial of life I had neglected myself, had not nurtured myself or loved and honored myself. I had been taught not to put myself forward but only to work hard and selflessly. I was on the wrong path.

***The Men's Group** presented the opportunity of sharing my life experience with diverse others in a non-blaming, supportive and non-critical and safe environment. I thrived, forgave myself, accepted myself, had time to explore issues with myself that were impossible to share elsewhere even in a relationship with a woman. I learnt about compassion and love as a result. My relationships outside the group have improved and my friendships within it enhanced.*

My Eulogy

Howard was my friend, and, up to his leaving this life my lover.

He gave me his family, his many other friends and all those who he came into contact so much... love, compassion, a joke, a drink, a dinner, an attentive and caring ear, wise advice, a helping hand, a constructive and practical idea.

At all times he pursued those values he held high, such as honesty, integrity and service of and to others.

Howard came from a loving home, and cared deeply for his family.

The trials of early youth, however, left Howard with a low self-esteem that he had to learn to replace with a connection to his Self.

He suffered much emotionally in his early years in the merchant navy, in relationships and in struggling to learn at a university college that he was good enough.

Howard was always and will always be 'Good Enough'.

He learnt this lesson well, with the humility, strength, gentleness and compassion for others he cared for, worked with and loved up to his death.

He was a naturally creative, disciplined and intelligent person, respected by his professional peers for his inventiveness, integrity, managerial competence and vision.

We will miss him and trust that by remembering him, his joy and humor of life, we will each take his example into our lives and honor him by pursuing our own growth now.

Ivan

Relationships

Relationships are about knowing or establishing my Self. What I really want from a relationship bothers me. At least this is a thought I have at the moment. My relationship with my mother, father and sisters seem a little empty. That doesn't mean I was deprived. I was taught to fend for myself and be brave, so things that hurt me when I was young I learnt to forget how I actually felt at the time, I think because no-one ever asked me how I felt about something if I was sad, so I never learnt to know how to express myself. We only dealt with things that were exciting or gave us a buzz. An example would be winning at something. Even that got a bit boring. My parents always worked long hours. So even to this day I have no real bond with them nor do my sisters. If my parents weren't home, neither was I. I was at a mate's place or working selling papers, delivering them or doing some other job. Meals were never regular and (from an early age) I could afford to buy my own.

So rejection is to me the thought of having to build up another relationship if I lost the only one I have at the moment with my wife and stepchildren. Because my wife didn't want any more children I think I missed the opportunity to feel close to anyone, closer than I feel now. Like I do have my wife, stepchildren and step-grandchildren but they may love me more than I them, because perhaps I have not learnt to love (although I am learning) as well as I should have. So I have built an automatic wall that comes up if there is rejection. I get hurt but only a little. I deal with it straight away, but I am more positive about changing my state of mind.

Cycles, Seasons and Tides

At this very time I feel I am getting to know my wife. I wonder why I didn't get to know her before, but I think it's because when I met my wife we had limited time together. I was in business working hard; my initial time with my wife was limited because she was already a mother of three. So I look back now and think I was trying to get to know all four people and making them part of my life. I just thought as long as I am a husband and do what a husband does, and do what a father does, I would be OK; do my duty.

It seems now I look back I've been an OK father, but I know that my wife and I fell in love and have survived on that feeling of being in love ever since, without fulfilling each other's needs. All our children have left home now, we have four grandchildren that come and stay, and I am now mature enough to read their faces and thoughts whereas I was too busy before, and, by the way, we get to hand them back to their parents, which leaves my wife and I alone again.

Initially when the children left, or rather the last one left (this year) my wife and I had trouble talking; we were trying to think of things to say to each other so the place/house wasn't so quiet. Now I am inquisitive about my wife. I am appreciating her more as a person. I can see more of that – her personality now, and I am absorbing every bit I can.

I've got a fair way to go still, but I'm working on it. It's like taking three steps forward and two back all the time. I seem to have done most things in reverse. I've had grandchildren at age 33 and experienced their babyhood; had young children at the age 24, and adults (as children) in my early 30s. But at age 42 I now almost feel equipped to be a father to my children. I love my wife differently now and it appears to be varying all the time.

Intimacy and Commitment

It has only been recently that I have realized (as silly as it sounds) to be totally committed to my relationship. Having said that ,I haven't got it right yet. My business has had my total commitment. That's why my business (which is something I always have felt I had to do) is successful. I had always assumed that if two people love each other and they work on the relationship, i.e. caring, being thoughtful, etc. that was all that was required. And, of course, providing for the family.

I haven't been able to experience total intimacy yet, as my wife (I think) has to deal with her past (mainly her childhood). Although lovable, sexy, etc. there is a barrier that she has to deal with yet and I have that feeling of either putting her in a position of being uncomfortable in some way if I push things. That's not to mention me being a perfectionist. I don't put things forward unless I can see the end result and how it is going to be achieved.

Looking Back

When I think about it, I wonder what is going to be invented next. I have seen some pretty amazing things in the first 40 years of my life. I am thinking what is going to become of people? There seems to be less work, more playtime, transport of all types to get you around, the scientific world/age is really upon us. I used to think it was pretty amazing.

The threat of violence is very evident throughout the world, yet people's knowledge of how to be at peace with one another is more prevalent. I guess there will always be wars of some sort; perhaps, the bad part of life exists so we can measure the good times. There was a saying I used to hear quite often 'When a country is finding things tough, a war of some sort will get the economy moving in some direction'. When wars end people will have the need to establish a life for themselves and become focused when all of the anger subsides. There are a lot of people out of work but few are devastated as most are out of work at this time.

Fathers

I learnt from my father that I could do anything I wanted to. I just had to decide what I wanted and do it. There were no boundaries. Be tough and you'll survive, don't cry.

I aspired to be like him because he was a very popular figure, a little larger than life. He cared for me when he felt guilty, I think, but didn't become a role model as a father. I only seem to have had a part-time father. He was there only when my mother insisted and persisted. I only learnt by asking questions, of which he always seemed to have most of the answers or a way of doing something I couldn't figure out. But from the age of seventeen or eighteen to nineteen I felt my father was more a mate; someone I knew and was happy to be around, but I don't think I knew him. My father never said he loved me, although I don't doubt he did (that generation of fathers just didn't say those things). Between the ages of twenty and twenty-one to twenty-four, I was travelling and didn't see my father much and from age 24 to 31 I only saw him twice as he split from my mother and was living in another state until he was killed in a plane crash.

I never knew how he felt about anything (a problem I have is expressing how I feel today sometimes). I wish he were around today, just to be able to speak to him and gain some of his wisdom. I now know my father was selfish, and I resented him in my mid-30s because I was also selfish (although in a different way).

The Movement of Men

Initially I was led to ***The Men's Group*** *via a threat of my marriage failing or rather just existing. It was recognized by people around me (and myself to an extent) that I personally had feelings within myself, unanswered questions, unanswered answers that I couldn't accept nor understand. I believe I was doing things 'right' in my life, but when there was a problem with what I thought was 'right' I was not handling it properly. I saw the problem different to what I should have because I wasn't in touch with myself. I came to the conclusion that I never understood why I thought what I was doing was 'right' in the first place. I realized that I was surviving. I had good intentions and most of my decisions to mend things came out okay, but I never quite knew why I took a particular path to solve a problem.*

I have learnt, from being involved in ***The Men's Group*** *(although it's been some time since I attended), that my problems are not isolated just to me. I found answers from others just by reflecting and listening to them. I'm not sure if I have that feeling of belonging yet, but that's a problem I have in most things. In fact, I think my feeling of not belonging is something that drives me in most things.*

My Eulogy

Ivan was born in the front room of the family house. He was always a very energetic boy who got up to a lot of mischief. He wasn't a bad kid, just very adventurous. Not afraid to try something new but very staid in his ways that he felt comfortable with.

As a young child to his late teenage years, Ivan was fairly aggressive.

He was a fighter, feared little, liked to always do things well, and have the respect of other kids and be recognized as a bit of a champion, but not over-expose anything that was done well. He just preferred everyone to know somehow.

He loved all types of sport and competitiveness, loved the big win, and was always keen to earn a quid. Bit of a smarty but reasonably well liked because through his teenage years he became a bit of a larrikin, although he studied hard at school.

He always worked as a youngster selling and delivering papers, or working any job that was going to buy him what he wanted. Fairly entrepreneurial most of his life he never did much more than he had to.

In his mid-teenage years he decided he wanted to be reasonably wealthy and that became a goal that consumed a large part of his time but he enjoyed it so it was no big deal. But to be wealthy for no particular reason other than to achieve the objective he never really had any respect for money as such.

He did a lot of travel throughout his whole life until he met and married his wife at age twenty-four. He became an instant family man of five and later a grandfather of four.

Jessie

Relationships

The hardest thing in a relationship for me is to be vulnerable and trusting and to have a prolonged period of intimacy. It's as if, when everything is going well, when joy, trust and love abounded, I need to pull back from the edge to withdraw from the commitment. This is if it becomes intolerable to be in a relationship that is so joyful and beautiful.

Cycles, Seasons and Tides

With my children near to the point of becoming independent and seeking their own ways in life, I am seeing a new relationship with my wife. With what I have learnt in the last few years with ***The Men's Group****, I can say I'm in the spring, a season with new growth. Exciting new pleasures and meanings to be found and relished.*

There is also a touch of fear because of the newness. This feeling is far outweighed by the excitement and joy.

Intimacy and Commitment

I had no feeling of intimacy with my mother or father. There was a feeling that this was 'wrong', that it was sinful. That one shouldn't be close to people. I had a feeling of rejection if I spoke of my problems. My mother would laugh or correct me. She also would not respect my privacy. So I learnt to not be intimate or confide in her of my pain or loves or love.

I have found in all my relationships, including that with my wife and children that I have been unable to have other than short periods of intimacy with any person.

Looking Back

Daily life at this time is exciting. It is and has been a time of great change. We have been liberated from the old Victorian restrictions of censorship of writing. People were able to read and see ideas and thoughts that were non-conformist. Clothing and behavior-patterns were less restrictive.

I saw work as my contribution to society, as a means of helping the society live as a unit and society repaid me with money to enable me to live and support my family. Work measured my day. It gave me purpose. I felt I contributed to the greater good of society. Work was one of my measures of my self-esteem. Work was also play for me. I got great satisfaction in the exactness of my work as well as the helping of people and the people contact.

The 80s and 90s were an exciting time to be alive. There had been great changes started in the late 60s and the 70s. These were carried through to the 80s and 90s.

I have reacted to many of the changes that were occurring initially with fear. What moved the changes lost me. What rights and freedoms moved I lost. My reaction to my wife going back to school to start a new profession was one of fear of the loss of my position in the family as the sole financial supporter. There was also a fear of failure of her new independence. I learnt with time to move from a co-dependent relationship to one of interdependence.

I saw the women's movement come with a rush. The freedom and equality of women became a reality for the first time. The equality of women was probably the greatest change in society. This brought on a new way of relationships between men and women. In this time, men are starting to look at themselves and the roles they have in partnerships, marriage and in the workplace. Men have begun to develop the feminine side of themselves and back out of the masculine macho, aggressive role they had adopted.

At the same time there is now a change in the way people are living. Society questions the so-called development of the earth and the damage that has been caused to the earth by man's exploitation of it.

This time has been exciting because of the ever-increasing change in attitudes, science, technology, politics, and human relations, communications. It is almost a period of chaos. The excitement is also accompanied by a fear of uncertainty. One certainly knows one is alive.

Fathers

I learned from my father to work and care for my wife and family, that my journey through life should be moral and ethical, and that my life should have integrity. My father was a caring man who cared for my mother, my sister and me. I learnt honesty and caring from my father.

Unfortunately, my father was not there for me. He was unable to be close and intimate. He was not there for me very often. I could not talk to him about the problems and difficulties I faced. He was a strict disciplinarian with a strong set of principles. He had love for us but had difficulty in showing it or saying it.

The Movement of Men

I joined initially and remain a member because I have no other place where I can talk and listen to men discuss intimate problems in an honest, caring and open way and where there is caring support from all present. I get companionship and care, trust and love from this group and constant insights into my life and myself. This is why I attend.

My Eulogy

Jessie was the first child of two.

He leaves a sister.

He attended university and attained a degree. After living for in London for 8½ years, he returned to Melbourne for the remainder of his life.

He was married in London, had four children, and he loved and cared deeply for his wife and his children.

He loved himself and was at peace with himself.

Jessie was a man who enjoyed life. He was vital and fun to be with.

He was a loving and caring man who worked hard to give his family the best he could.

He was a man who enjoyed life, who was vital, fun to be with, imaginative and innovative, loving and caring.

He learnt with time to be intimate.

He spent a lot of time and effort giving his family the best quality of life possible.

This was however at the cost of being with his family.

In the latter years he learnt how much he had missed by not being part of the family and just the provider.

His change of 'being' brought great joy to his life.

He developed a spiritual side to his life in later years.

Jessie died a happy man, interested in learning to the very end.

Kent

Relationships

The most difficult aspect of a relationship for me is the expectation that my partner should be perfect in every way, even though I know that it just can't be so. I suppose that it is my own desire for a perfect world that I seek perfection in my partner. I want my partner to be the source of all my satisfaction, the cure of all my ills. I want my relationship to be easy, and I want my partner to not be just who she is but to possess every desirable aspect of every other woman.

My difficulty in relationship stems from viewing my relationship from what is not there, rather than living the marvelous experiences that I share with my partner.

Cycles, Seasons and Tides

Whenever I'm asked to visualize an earthly image, like the sea or mountains or the sky, the one recurring image that always comes to mind is that of a river setting. I imagine myself sitting on the bank of a river on a warm beautiful day. Tall trees along both sides of the bank, through which a river, ever so calm and still, reflects back the image of the trees, grass and sky. A simple, wave much like a large ripple, moves through the river, causing little disturbance to the rest of the water as it moves from the distance towards me, then in front of me, and then slowly passes me, as it moves silently forward into the distance.

I feel like that wave. I feel as though I am moving through life, not disturbing the world about me, but peacefully experiencing the beauty of the scene I've just described. I don't know what lies ahead, and it hurts to not know. I cannot go back, but yet, there is a sense of wholeness as the momentum of the wave moves forward to other places.

Intimacy and Commitment

I am often reluctant to talk and behave intimately with my wife because I don't believe that I can truly express my feelings without hurting her. My feelings and views don't often match her views. Her indignations, criticisms and the sadness she expresses when she hears what I say destroy the opportunity to be intimate. It's as though I need to be intimate with her in ways that are only positive. She only likes to hear my 'good feelings', or those feelings and views that are safe and which don't hurt her. I find this 'selective intimacy' ultimately dishonest to myself. I don't like behaving that way, so I keep quiet, distant and safe.

Looking Back

I hope that when you read these words, that you will appreciate my experience of life, as a young man. I'm soon to become a father, in a few months in fact. So you may be interested in knowing how I feel about becoming your father/grandfather/great grandfather. It is both exciting and daunting. I'm looking forward to the arrival of my first baby into the family. I'm frightened of the responsibility that that entails. I've always considered myself to be a son, rather than a 'father'. So, somehow it makes me feel 'old', not in a frail, ageing and tired sense, but rather one where I am no longer 'young', no longer a 'small boy' wanting to be like his father.

I am also afraid that I will not pay enough attention to you; that I'll be busy working or studying and that I'll miss the joy of watching and helping you grow. I'm scared that I will be like many fathers, a supporter and breadwinner, but someone who plays no real emotional role in your life. Knowing my father did the best that he could, I know it is up to me to take my family relationships further into the emotional realm, to instill into my children my happiness and joy. I hope that you all love your lives like I've tried to do.

Fathers

My father always taught me to be independent and strong. To love my family and use them for support in life. He always encouraged me to aspire to high standards in school and work. I always love the presence of my father. We often have little to talk about that is of little meaning, although we can talk for long periods on 'safe' issues like what to look for in buying a car.

I know that my father behaved in ways that were expected of his generation, and I cherish the dreams, the independence he has instilled in me, but I would have dearly loved to go away with my father (and not anyone else) on excursions like camping and fishing. But unfortunately my father did not like such activities. It would have been wonderful for him to show me how to set up a tent or a fishing line, or repair the car (although he did teach me to ride a bike and drive a car). But what he taught me did not prepare me for the world. They were not enough. I wanted more activities like these. I want the memories of a life with my father, rather than just someone who supported the household, but with little personal contact.

The Movement of Men

Some years ago I became conscious of my life. I had, for a long time, even as far back as my early childhood, recognized that people lacked the ability to live honestly with themselves. I took part in this dishonesty, without realizing the negative and destructive effects it had on my life. I lacked the ability to 'link up' emotionally with family, friends and work peers.

Eventually, I realized that these destructive processes just could not go on. ***The Men's Group*** *offers a fantastic experience. It enables me to link up and connect with people, particularly men.*

My Eulogy

Kent was born into a family that encouraged close relationships with other family members, but less so with the other people in his community.

He was always encouraged to mix with family, and behave in the ways expected of his Italian traditions.

Consequently, his childhood years were spent devoted to his family; they were happy years.

But little time was given to developing himself.

It was only later, in his adolescence that he recognized his own wishes to discover and experience life.

Yet the energy and the bravery to break out were not present.

It was not until his mid-twenties, when he met his future wife, that he confronted his feelings.

Looking back, Kent always tried to be 'fair'.

He disliked the dishonesty he saw in people and vehemently rejected people who appeared dishonest in his life.

Lester

Relationships

Rejection and the betrayal of trust are, for me, what it is like being in relationship and is the way I know myself in the world. Relationships are like a mirror of paradoxes. It is like love, a projection of all aspects of myself. I don't always get what I expect (perhaps we never, in the end, get what we expect). Perhaps when I let go into this, I get more than I expect. Without having a relationship I cannot know myself. Without rejection I cannot grow.

As a small child I felt at the center of my/the world. Gradually, through my parents' criticism and rejection I grew to know that I am only a small part of things. I have started on my journey towards grace and individuation. Without relationships and their failure I could not do this. Relationships are the boat I travel in, over and through the sea of the spirit.

Cycles, Seasons and Tides

My life is running like a full tide, a great forward surge.

The cycle is in the ascendancy of early summer and the fruit is set and ready to ripen.

Intimacy and Commitment

Intimacy and commitment are mirrors of paradox. When women say that the men or the man in their lives fear intimacy and/or commitment I ask myself 'Why does this woman not trust herself? Why can she not commit herself and show intimacy? Has she been so betrayed in the past? Her father?' I have to remember that she also is on a journey of knowing herself. That she also looks into the mirror and sees what she fears. Then I may ask myself, 'What is it about me that she feels she cannot trust or commit to?'

Looking Back

My dear Grandson,

I bring you from the past my love and wishes of well-being. Life for me has been good and it appears it will continue so. We live in a relatively peaceful world. Although there is still much suffering in the world at large, there continues to be a growing number of people committed to making it a better place.

One of the most positive and interesting things that has occurred around this time has been the development and identification of the 'Men's Movement'. With growing enthusiasm we men have followed the invitation/opportunity opened up to us by the women so many years ago. Men are learning to put aside their greed and brutish side and to love themselves first so that they may be loved and give love to others.

I am certain that it will be the same for you. That is, that you will come to know that we are in the world to get to know ourselves, to live our lives and to love and nurture others dear to us. I give to you my wholehearted love. The future is yours. Nurture it with enthusiasm and loving care.

Your Grandad,

xoxo

Fathers

From my father I learned self-respect, confidence and love. He was a 'gentleman' in the real sense of the word. I honored and loved him in life and death. My father taught me to love nature, to love materials and how to work with them. He taught me the joy of stroking and touching a beautiful piece of wood before you worked on it. He gave me a real tool kit when I was about six years old. He gave me freedom through his trust of me.

What I didn't receive from my father that I would have loved is to have known him even better and to have been able to spend more time with him than I did. He also taught me some things that have not been so good, such as, 'that if a job is worth doing, it is worth doing properly'. The perfectionist. This I now have a perspective on and do not blame him for. When I experience or am in contact with the war he fought in I become very emotional and grieve for his pain at that time.

The Movement of Men

Being part of a men's group for me is like being a surfer on a board in a huge sea. It is like being carried forward upon a great wave of surging and sparkling experiences and emotions. A great wave that can be deep and green of unknown depths and sudden dissolution; sometimes dumping one onto the sand and leaving one high and dry.

Sometimes it presents me with pure terror; at other times it embraces me in gentleness. It always has a natural order about it and fulfills a fundamental need in me as a man.

My Eulogy

Lester was a good man, a good teacher.

Like the rock, he was there when he was needed.

He had a fortunate life full of many blessings and few disasters.

His childhood was stable and loving and as he often said 'full of sunshine'.

When he was 15 or 16 he was 'launched' into the adult world by his parents; feeling good about himself and loved by them, although very shocked by the rudeness of the change.

His father was mostly right!

Lester has throughout most of his life been an artist who had followed his own path.

He had rarely been part of the mainstream but has spoken from the heart to the heart in others in his work.

He has left behind a number of humble yet valued expressions of his journey in the form of public sculptures.

Martin

Relationships

The hardest thing in relationships for me is not being heard, which is the wider aspect of not actually ever been seen for myself and allowed to be myself, both positive and negative. In dealing with women, the pain of watching them attack not because of what has occurred between us but rather their failure to control or mold me into what they think I should be. It is also difficult for me to see through what I see as the artifice, image or front of women's words and actions to discern, love and respect the 'real' them.

The lack of honesty and the desire to maintain beliefs without questioning whether they are accurate hurts, as well as the cowardice at real confrontation and vulnerability as women busily protect themselves. The feeling of being used or being seen as an object, not someone who is loved and respected for Self but rather something to be used and discarded.

Rejection hurts but the above manner of rejection hurts most because it never gives a chance at reconciliation of the pain between people and leaves open wounds. Criticism hurts but does not wound provided it is fair and constructive and not meaning to wound. Women don't fight fair but expect or demand that men fight fair and protect them but only when they choose. This double standard leaves out honesty and hurts everyone.

Criticism, Blame, Sarcasm and Accusation

I listen to it in the belief that I might learn if it is presented in a soft manner. I don't listen to it if is presented in anger. I withdraw, become empty inside, and feel disconnected, very alone, unsafe and fearful. I listen to it; try to see it as real or unreal about either a situation or myself. How I react is dependent on who does it (e.g., a friend commenting is different from a boss). It hurts me the majority of the time, and depending on the level of fatigue, I react with anger if very tired. If well, I give tit for tat. Basically, it hurts me and I defend myself.

Cycles, Seasons and Tides

I am in winter, with a hint of spring and although I dislike winter I am happy that it's here. It has been a bleak, hard winter that truly in the past months has been relieved by a series of warm 'Chinooks' that have given short but much needed warmth. I am grateful for that warmth.

Maybe spring will be better, warmer at least. Hope, peace of mind and a sense of belonging have been absent during this winter. I see my life as not just one set of seasons but as a set of many seasons. Whereas in the past the expectations of set, unpleasantly hot summers was that they were followed by long isolating cold winters was the norm and the death would have been the logical end of them. In this winter something has changed and if not hope but rather the desire for hope has come into being. Physical warmth is matched with emotional warmth and whereas my body needs the tropics to feel unencumbered my spirit needs so much less to feel expanded by emotional warmth.

The tide is coming in, receding, and I am no longer continually swamped and needing to just stay afloat. Soon I will swim again. People drown in both shallow and deep water but mainly shallow.

Intimacy and Commitment

Intimacy requires trust and in my experience women break that trust without thinking about it. However, if something is expressed in confidence to a woman she will respect that confidence. Females seem to have contempt for men, and an attitude of 'we know best' is expressed in that confidence-breaking.

For a man intimacy means a sharing of all hopes and fears, positive and negative, of the past, present and future. To a woman, intimacy is only hearing what she wishes to hear. If a man is actually honest he is penalized or attacked and the subject changed. Most people (men and women) are self-listening when they are fearful and real intimacy is super risk-taking and therefore fear-provoking.

Commitment is about meeting a woman's (primary) fantasy and a man giving up his (primary) fantasy. Commitment is only asked if the male has arrived or achieved or is in the process of achieving. Female commitment is to meet her fantasy. It's become my experience that both parties don't get their needs met, only their fantasies.

Looking Back

What excites me as a man are feelings of creativity and learning: first in my work after burnout, in the wonders, peace and beauty of nature and becoming a part of it, and a return of health and then an increase in physical well-being so that both the environment I lived in and my physical health were one and the same.

The fears for the time we live in were the fears of lack of direction and a sense of loss of certain hopes and beliefs, fears of relationship and the ambivalence about the nature of that relationship. The relationship that followed and how I was attracted to both the pain and the dysfunction in others and vice-versa, in contrast to the attraction of health with a new woman. Fear of illness brought by years of ill health and the lack of energy to even achieve anything positive, the fear that I would never get well and the desire to finish the pain, and the fear of double-standards so ingrained as to be automatic to both sexes that left people dealing viciously with each other. And being both the victim and the victimizer through misunderstanding and misinterpretation. Fear of being a victim, thinking as a victim and therefore self-righteously victimizing so I would never be victim again. Continuing the cycle. Hope that breaking the silence would challenge false beliefs in my Self and others.

Fathers

I learnt not to bring troubles/failures home, to settle them myself and not to ask for or expect any help. What I learnt from my father was he who wins unites the history and that history becomes fact. Also I learnt to love questioning what is around me, to look past what is offered to what is really happening. To observe and listen without being a part of what is happening. To be an outsider has its value.

I learnt that anger between those who love can be constructive and if used assertively lead to confrontation so that there can be reconciliation. I learnt that I should never let people know what I am thinking, not to make myself vulnerable. 'Be friendly to all, trust in no one.' That I have only myself to depend on at all times.

I also learnt to accept being alone: 'That those you love the most, can hurt you the most'; the Sicilian proverb 'Where there is death, there is hope.'

What I would have loved from my father was time, direction and attention. He was not there for me; he could not be for he was busy providing for his family.

The Movement of Men

I have had experience of groups that shared a common experience and how discussing their feelings and experiences had given members of that group reduction of isolation, a sense of belonging, support in dealing with that common experience in many different ways. Basically groups become awareness/conscience-raising experiences in a safe environment. So when I realized that a men's group was available I thought I would experiment and try it.

Being in a men's group gives me a safe environment to discuss issues that are not macho/politically correct in the 'real' world where the first rule is if 'politically correct', don't question it. To me it removes the sense of isolation that has been occurring inside myself when I examine and question certain beliefs. It is a sense of belonging.

My Eulogy

Martin was a man who was sometimes there when called upon for love, friendship and fun. The majority of the time, however, he was just going through the motions of being present.

He was born in Carlton, raised in North Melbourne and Flemington and educated in Catholic primary and secondary schools.

At university he met his wife and may have married her as a result of faulty birth control and over indulgence in alcohol.

They never settled down after this event and he was very immature and resistant to/of mainstream society.

He was a loner.

Eventually he did psychiatric nursing and completed it with the use of much input.

After a couple of years of nursing he left for Asia and there fulfilled life as a beach bum, the only ambition he ever had which was not borrowed from others.

Returning to Melbourne he cleaned up his act, returned to nursing and died soon afterward.

Noel

Relationships

The hardest thing to deal with in relationships for me is to be caught up in the ongoing argument that comes with the assumption of archetypal roles. This might seem a contradiction because even being in a relationship is playing these roles.

Certainly, criticism and rejection are lurking around and highlighting my fears. But in dealing with the projections that come from my partner and in dealing with the projections that I give to my partner the greatest loss for me is the loss of INTIMACY.

I feel that when I am caught up in the process of conflict I have lost contact with myself and am made powerless by it. I also know that I am dealing with some of my unresolved issues in this process and I have to go through to their resolution. I just wish I could go straight to it, get in touch with my feelings and express my fears.

Cycles, Seasons and Tides

I feel that I am constantly in spring. I feel that in the winters of my life the experiences had made me adopt many layers for protection and to dull my senses. Now, as I allow myself to discover these layers and discard them. I am reborn over and over again. I am blossoming with each new freedom. I am increasingly sensing the vulnerability that enhances my experience of my life.

Intimacy and Commitment

I wish to express directly without editing what I am feeling, where I am hurting, what my wants are and what needs I am trying to satisfy. I wish to feel powerful in the expression of my innermost fears. I wish to be understood and accepted without qualification. I wish to understand myself through the most intimate connection with my Self and others. I wish to communicate without fear.

Sometimes I withhold communication and I am surprised that it is or was not a conscious decision. I wish I could be aware of this at the time. I realize that my fears cloud this awareness.

Looking Back

Life physically seems and is very comfortable. All of my basic needs of food, clothing, shelter are well catered for. The search for material possessions and financial security are a preoccupation and a distraction. It is a good and safe time for families. Family units still exist and thrive generally. Children are able to aspire to and achieve basically whatever they desire.

The time I live in is a privileged time to live in. Most of the drudgery of life has been eliminated for those who live in Western society. It is a great time for self-examination. People are looking to free themselves from traditional values and standards and for ways to free themselves from their self-imposed limitations.

I am excited about providing something better and more honest for myself. I am excited about the possibilities of immediate implementation of my creativities. I am excited about the greater interactivity with computers and the new horizons they have opened. I am worried about the breakdown of society and the atrocities that man still inflicts on man. I have a belief that man is destroying the earth through trying to conquer it. I fear the loss of my individual ability to make decisions that would save the world and the things that matter to me.

Fathers

I learned from my father not to give myself approval. I learned to escape through abusing my body and dulling my senses through addictions. I learned to be non-communicative. I learned to be kind and generous. I learned to be afraid of decision-making and implementation. I learned to live in my head from my father. I learned to not deserve what I had and what I wanted. I learned to give away my power and my freedom.

I would have loved to have my father's approval and recognition. I would have loved my father to be able to tell me what he was feeling. I would have loved my father to show me how to be fearless in my communication. I would have loved my father to show me how to have fun. I would have loved my father to give me a sense of belonging. I would have loved my father to show me how to be strong and fearless in the world. I would have loved my father to say he loved me enough to love himself.

The Movement of Men

I found I was in crisis in my relationship and I had lost touch with myself. I was lost in a materialistic search and even though I felt in control I was escaping intimacy with my Self, my partner and my family. I didn't know what was happening. To be in a men's group initially provided me with an awareness that other men were experiencing almost identically similar problems. I found I was limited profoundly by my own experience. Listening to other men speak was like listening to the story of my own life except that I was removed one step and could get a different perspective that allowed some more objectivity.

Whenever I had a problem I could always guarantee that the men's group discussions, no matter what the topic was, would produce a shift that would change or dissolve the problem.

My Eulogy

Noel was a man who never seemed happy with himself.

He always seemed to be carrying a heavy load. He looked like he was carrying the responsibility for the world.

He was too selfless, not selfish enough.

He continually gave away his power because he found it difficult to define and then to deserve his wants.

He was kind and lovable and good to be around.

He was too nice and wished to be more powerful than that.

He was a good father and a supportive husband and people might sometimes feel sadness when they identify with the way he saw himself.

He always found it difficult to take what he needed to find peace and so he sabotaged himself in the most powerful yet subtle ways.

He loved his family.

He desperately wanted to express his feelings and to give himself approval.

Oliver

Relationships

The hardest thing for me is to open up and put out when all I want to do is withdraw into myself. For me this flows from a fear of rejection. When my partner is not giving me what I want, or responding to me in a positive way I get angry. That anger is generally expressed as withdrawal. By withdrawing I can protect myself and also hurt the other person by showing them that I can get along all right without them. This withdrawal then feeds on itself as my partner then treats me less and less how I want to be treated.

The hardest thing is to avoid going into this downward destructive cycle or when in it, break out. The only way to break out is to open up. But even when I know this, it is very hard to do. For me this behavior-pattern is one of my greatest challenges and it is fed on fear of rejection. To protect myself from rejection I withdraw.

Cycles, Seasons and Tides

I am in the depths of winter with a fierce blizzard blowing. I am facing enormous competitive pressures at my work. To survive I would normally assume that I need to be as ruthless as those trying to attack me. However, I do not really wish to do that. What I wish to do is withdraw from these areas of work that are the target of competition from colleagues and move to create other niches that are not occupied. In doing this I am nevertheless struck by the concern of my ego; will my colleagues perceive me as weak for not fighting over what they want?

Underpinning them I have confidence that it will work itself out. The issue is finding the will and commitment to state the course and create the role other than just throwing it all in. This has all impacted on my family and the good news is that in the past I would have bottled all these tensions up and withdrawn. Now, at least I have been able to try and tell my wife how I feel.

Intimacy and Commitment

I do not think I have ever been totally intimate with my partner. To be totally intimate would be to share everything that I feel. My fears in sharing everything are twofold: (1) it places me totally in my partner's hands exposed; (2) I am not sure my partner will appreciate/accept all of my feelings as they relate to her.

The other practical reality is that to be intimate my partner must be in touch with her emotions in order to be able to express them. I find this difficult. Intimacy is the lifeblood of a relationship. Without it we cannot go forward together.

Looking Back

The great thing about the time I am living in is that the choices available are almost infinite… a myriad of pleasures, ways to have fun, and things to spend money on, etc. The great irony is that the greater the choices, the more we moved from the simple things that are the essence of life. In many ways these times have become devoid, empty, as we increasingly fill our lives with the peripheral. However, as the emptiness grew it forced me to consider how to get back in touch with myself and with those whose company I valued.

The fear is that if one stops being on a treadmill, competing for each step up the ladder of success, pursuing a path which one thinks is what a man should be. If one stops this pursuit and seeks comfort in oneself and sharing emotionally, that one will not service in the society that is the 80s and 90s.

Fathers

My father was able to show me what determination and individualism were. He gave me a strong sense of doing my best. He taught me to talk intimately at one level, talk about emotions and feelings but from the intellect, not the heart. He gave me a point of reference for my own identity as head of our family and also a part of a broader family.

What I never received from my father was an understanding of how to be with a woman, what a loving relationship with a woman was and could look like. I never received his undivided time. Generally our time together was placed between other commitments.

The Movement of Men

I come to the group to hear how other men talk about the emotions that affect us all as men. I come to the group to find a reference point to hear other men's experiences and to share my experiences. It has been a challenging and very supportive experience. To hear men talk about deep emotions, share painful experiences and contribute to the discussion has provided great comfort that I can do that without fear. Without fear because what is said is received without judgment and also because the spectrum of what is said shows how much we all have the same problems.

I feel somewhat liberated, as I always feared coming to a men's group. Now I have been and not only survived but benefited greatly from the experience. I am also personally stronger in pursuing my relationship with my wife, kids and friends. I can express my feelings/emotions.

My Eulogy

Oliver lived a full life that encompassed family, work and friends.

He provided solid support for people and friends in need.

Oliver enjoyed sport, traveling, relaxing with family and friends.

Underneath these active pursuits Oliver really welcomed the opportunity to share experiences and emotions.

Whilst this was never easy for Oliver, he spent a lot of his life working and searching for ways to share/connect with people.

The relationship with his wife went through difficult times but their underlying commitment to share has enabled their relationship to grow.

This was also reflected in the relationship Oliver has had with his children.

In his personal life Oliver was also content.

In his work and professional life he succeeded on his own terms and was true to who he was as a person.

Parker

Relationships

Without a doubt, criticism and rejection are the hardest things to deal with in relationships. Just recently I allowed another person to get to know me and I allowed myself to be vulnerable and shared openly with her what I was experiencing to the best of my ability at the time.

The hardest thing I have ever had to do was exposing who I thought and felt I was or I am. As I was going through this process my mind went solid and rigid and stiff, my legs went like jelly although my calf and thigh muscles were as hard as a rock, I had butterflies in the belly and I became very ill. I tried so, so, so hard not to run away. But the strain I felt on the true Self became too much for me and I felt as though I needed to go away and rest in a comfort zone that I have developed both consciously and subconsciously in my life. I have tried not to give myself anymore of a hard time over this happening although it has been difficult. In summary the hardest thing in relationships for me is to get honest and expose myself.

Cycles, Seasons and Tides

I believe I am just completing the spring and the rebirth and I am entering the summer and experiencing with no mind-altering substances. I welcome this time but feel very anxious. I do not feel lost or lonely for in the springtime I have been learning. I learned and developed some abilities that enable me to re-connect with my Self and higher self. Some of these abilities are rituals, meditation, prayer and openness, honesty, trust, action and acceptance.

Intimacy and Commitment

Commitment is for me (based on experience of losses in my life)... almost impossible. It hurts me too much when somebody goes away. Intimacy reminds me that I am not good enough, and if I am not good enough a partner they won't like me, and she will go away. And that hurts like hell. I am sorry to myself for being like this and I pray to a God for my own understanding that this can and will continue to change.

Looking Back

In these years, son, I am scared, frightened and excited. I'm going through a journey and meeting other men on a similar journey, questioning what it is like for them to be a man in life, in a relationship and in the world we live in. I have gained insight into my fears and found that one fear had been motivating me, taking choice away from me and suspending me from moving. Financial insecurity is everywhere around me but I don't believe I have suffered from that for I believe in myself to truly love myself.

I protect myself very carefully and cunningly against trickery and move around alone finding many beautiful places less stressful. Being alone was what gave me well-being and developing abilities to regain my free choice into myself and the end result was peace of mind. What great strengths I have experienced. I truly love what I will call the years of the learning curve.

Fathers

My father taught me how to improvise and to create, how to be a physical worker and how not to be a 'whinger' and dwell but to put action into my life.

I did not learn from Dad how to express my feelings or how to treat a lady or how to interact with a female. I wish that my father could have taught me that.

P.S Became a protector of women no matter what that cost myself. I don't like seeing women hurting. It distresses me.

The Movement of Men

*I came to **The Men's Group** because my interaction with other people, especially females, was not very good and I felt on the inside as though I did not truly trust or want to be like that any longer. In a men's group the sharing, caring and connecting and interaction with other men helped me identify what negates me from being able to connect with myself and therefore have difficulty in exposing on an honest level with others especially females whom I cannot and I could not ever have experienced true intimacy, if I did not have any idea who I was or what was happening with myself.*

I thank Paul Mott and the other men for their honesty over the years, in them sharing their lives with me for my life, as I now know it today.

My Eulogy

Parker was scared and frightened as a child.

He rebelled during his school days and isolated himself.

He would put on a brave front and try to please his father.

He loved his mother but he felt he never got to experience her love once she started to drink.

This to Parker caused a great hole in the soul, which for years he tried to fill.

But the ways in which he tried to fill this space became dangerous and detrimental to his well-being, almost killing him.

It was as a result of the whole experience of going to the doors of insanity and death that his life changed to one of being a spiritual inward journey with no end; hence naming himself 'Never Ending Story'.

He went through enormous change in this time in three areas; mentally, physically and spiritually and he wanted everybody who cared to know that before he died he experienced freedom from the bounds of self.

He tried, when appropriate, to pass his experience on to others but found enormous difficulty in doing this and decided to let go and let God do this.

His message was that 'I am with myself now'.

Rest now, Parker.

Quincy

Relationships

There are a few things I find difficult. One is being a question of tenure. Relationships always seem to end on me usually quickly. Then start afresh with a blaze of hope and glory, thence petering out in the usual manner. It seems I go into relationships with unspecified intentions and little expectations.

I am also very selfish in relationships. I also get to a certain point where both my Self and my partner are opening up to possibilities, mostly positive, and I either destroy them or am incapable to carry them through. It seems at the point of just before leaving a relationship when I'm in self-questioning mode, I feel helpless, rudderless, completely out of my depth and without any wisdom to rely on (both instilled or experienced). At that point I believe I'm in a very juvenile space. Most times I wish difficulties to arise (and even create them) in order to give me a reason to leave (or mistreat) a relationship.

Cycles, Seasons and Tides

My life feels like it is in a transient stage. There is little solidarity and much changeability. Sometimes it (life) feels like the warmth of spring and the freshness that season also brings. At other times, I feel an impending mood of autumn. Impending meaning that something darker and colder may happen, something like a winter in terms of duration and mood.

The only consistency I have at the moment is changeability. Though in these changes there is optimism and hope. It is just that the shackles of imprisonment that once bound me are hard to keep off. It is hard to keep negative thoughts and actions out of myself when they have been part of a staple diet for so long.

Healthy changes planted recently have started to prosper slowly flowering in a spring season. It is my duty to keep a natural procession of seasonal change in order. By that I mean I have to let my life be, let it prosper naturally, let the seasons flow and the tide take me where I need to go.

Intimacy and Commitment

It is mainly difficult for me because I am always in judgment. Is this the right woman to commit to/to be totally intimate with? Therefore I am a little committed/intimate to all women I meet. But that is all it is, a little committed. It probably stems from a dominant mother always in total judgment of the female company I keep. In other words she has her choices for me. It has obviously affected me almost subliminally so that I have broken away from the family. I have come to see problems, yet I still sometimes get entangled.

Looking Back

The earlier times I have lived in were certainly hedonistic times for me, mainly a blur of substances and work and travelling. At this time of my life things are a little more refined. Even to the effect that I have to catch my breath and analyze what happened earlier. Whereas my well-being when I was younger was completely dependent on what woman/substance I was doing, now my well means being physically nice to myself. Well-being is being a well self, not totally selfish, as I was earlier in my life. Maybe caring more is a better way to put how I am now.

Work used to be my self-justification, my mirror, my conductor for views and actions like clothes... something I could wear on the outside to show the world who I was. Work then, as much as possible, became a facet (albeit, an important one) of my life, not the controlling force. It was not the reason I woke for. Work became just another way to express myself… another way of self-actualizing. My type of work could physically drain me, so it was important to stay fit and active. Work begot fitness and fitness begot work. Mostly, what I got from work is satisfaction, as long as I continued to learn.

Fears when I was younger were fears of not having enough money. I don't know what for but not enough to spend I suppose. Also fears that the feeling of self-indulgence may end and then what do we do? Fears now are physical for: getting older, bringing more risks. Life now for me is a matter of improving odds and taking different risks. Risk Management I think it's called.

Fathers

Sometimes I just wondered where you were in my youth. And I also wonder why you weren't there. I mean what did I do wrong as a five year old? How could I be the innocent recipient of your past problems? I really don't think I deserved that. What I needed was some of your time, some of your love, and somebody I could call my father.

I did receive some of your affability and charm and a certain amount of your style. It would also be said I received part of your sharp wit. Though I must say I copped a fair amount of your fearful tendencies (though I must say I have beaten most of them). I have not only picked up your addictive characteristics but also the ability to get on top of them… such a perfect irony.

The Movement of Men

This particular men's group reminds me that when I'm struggling and feel 'alone' in thoughts, that there are other men feeling much the same. When I listen to other men and hear problems/beliefs I realize how petty most of the world's actions are. Right in the circle you see things where they really lie. Things we speak about here are of the utmost importance. They are the relevance and sometimes are the roots for actions in the world.

The circle is a cradle of thoughts. It is both new and ancient. It is as fine and wise as the participants involved. It is a truth in itself. I invariably get what I need when I participate in the group.

My Eulogy

Quincy was a man who had an enormous zest for life.

He was a man who could seize the day and shake it for all it was worth.

He was also an ambitious man who achieved a lot but also sometimes set great, almost unachievable goals.

It did not matter that he may not have achieved all things.

For him the thrill of the chase was in everything.

His capacity for life was shown in his love and his loved ones.

Most people raised their own expectations and ambitions in his company.

He was a leader and honest worker with a fine work ethic.

He also had fine artistic talents, probably not explored enough in his short life.

Over his latter years that 'artist' temperament cooled and formed into a more peaceful acceptance of his Self. This energy was immense and through application generally achieved what he wished to achieve.

He leaves us in peace.

Ralph

Relationships

The hardest thing in a relationship is learning to take responsibility for my own needs. This requires me to identify issues, accept that I have needs and that I am not self-sufficient, and creatively go about fulfilling them. If I fail to take responsibility for my own needs and I blame my partner first, such as if I can't cope with a situation and I find fault with her where previously there was no problem, then my eyes are closed. If left, this can fester in my imagination and my ego starts to think that it may be more satisfying in another relationship, or by abandoning the relationship I am in. At this point I start to hurt. In not dealing with this issue in a truthful way, I do not take responsibility for myself and my basic needs.

If I'm quick and focused I deal with this stuff, which being in a relationship has served up to me. I get wisdom and feel good. If I'm not quick, I hurt more and more till I do face the issue. Losing sight of what's my stuff and what belongs to the other party brings a confusion with it that leads to struggle and conflict about superficial aspects of life. Being clear about my own self-deceptions, limitations and strengths, enables me to enter into a relationship. This is the hardest requirement of a relationship. The more I come to know my Self the easier the relationship becomes.

Cycles, Seasons and Tides

Winter is a time of meditation, the using of energy, nutrients stored to prepare myself for rapid expressions of growth during spring. I've been preparing for spring for quite a few years. I believe the time for bearing fruit is at hand.

The wisdom I've accumulated wants to explore the real experience of the unfolding flower to see the color, to smell the scent, to taste the fruit. Life seems so full of possibilities of no longer just doing things, but to produce from deeper buds of connectedness.

Intimacy and Commitment

Commitment and intimacy require emotional risk, high risk. It is hard to believe that taking the plunge and risking ego could connect us to enlightenment. My inclination is to avoid the plunge and to live out life in terms of what I know, which is usually oriented to the cognitive world for doing things like, building houses, using machines, etc. Being safe.

Journeying to the emotional center, becoming connected with the different parts of my masculine/feminine self, enabling a connectedness with the emotional center of a woman has been a very difficult journey for me. And I believe most men I've met or have known have found this. At a very young age I was on this journey, but got sidetracked. I'm so pleased to be back on track.

Looking Back

My enjoyment and well-being-ness revolves around my personal relating. My wife and I have a loving relationship where we know and experience each other's growth and struggle. Our personal lives interact with our involvement with the natural environment. The seasons are important to our lives. As gardeners and farmers we appreciate our dependency on the providence of another nature. We both get great enjoyment seeing our attempts to make things grow and bear fruit.

My fears in the times I am living are mainly to do with the fact that people who exercise leadership in society show startling ineptitude about the relation between people and the environments. Only occasionally do governments seem to be in touch with the things that will truly benefit mankind. I doubt that putting vast resources into developing casinos for gambling, and as debt-solving measures will benefit people in any way.

People generally are turning to try and reconnect with parts of themselves and others in a more spiritual way. They are realizing the poverty of such a focus on external gain. I hope by 2050 this trend has produced further gains for people.

Fathers

I learned very strong moral convictions about how to be a decent human being: responsible, honest to the core, full of humanity.

I didn't learn how to mediate the above, how not to feel responsible for everything that was wrong with the world and others. I didn't learn to be caring enough about my own over-loading of personal responsibility. I didn't learn to be responsible for my own health.

I learned to be very skillful in practical tasks, a very lateral person of many skills, not restricted by boundaries. I learned to do things for myself and became very confident in most areas except that of mixing socially. I wish he'd been able to teach me to be at ease with my emotions and with my interactions with people. I learned to be very self-sufficient, but not to let others in to share my space. I wish he'd taught me to utilize support mechanisms outside of my Self and the family. I've learned to love my father and others around me; perhaps he taught me more than I realize.

The Movement of Men

I came to ***The Men's Group*** *because I found I wasn't making emotional connections with people and with men in particular. I had no confidence in men; I had largely given up on the masculine both within others and myself. As I became interested in regenerating this vital part of myself, I also looked to other men for assistance and explorations of what maleness could be in its positive manifestations. About the time I was looking and wondering how to deal with this male question, Paul asked me to come along. As I began to discover more meaningful relations with people, it became apparent that such interactions could enrich my whole life. The possibilities were endless, and I felt very certain that joining the men's group would be an important step to take.*

I have really learnt to connect with men. I hear stories in the group similar to my own. I hear people struggling with issues, blackness, joys, etc. just like I do and I know I'm really not by myself; I'm part of a family.

My Eulogy

Ralph was a man of strong convictions.

At times he pursued his beliefs too intensely, creating tension.

On the whole he learned to achieve a balanced perception of his own self, his friends and the world around him.

He learned to know himself and to harmonize within, creating a very peaceful and tolerant personality, one that loved and enjoyed.

This allowed others to enjoy a harmony in their relations with him.

This is the Ralph we are here to remember and honor.

One of the things that brought Ralph great happiness was when he felt he contributed to the growth and happiness of those around him and those whom he loved.

To contribute to the growth of another meant he had a surplus of good feeling deep within to truly share the space of another's life and well-being was a goal he lived for, as he generated harmony and love within himself.

This goal was a struggle at times, having a vision bigger than his capacity.

But Ralph learned that there is strength in realizing his own limitations and the sanctity of humbleness.

We will miss you, Running Water, and look forward to meeting you in the next world.

Scott

Relationships

My experience of being in relationships is not being heard, or appreciated, being used as the dumping ground for my partner's unresolved issues. Being held responsible for my partner's feelings. Not being trusted enough by my partner to allow herself to be vulnerable with me. I have a sense that there is no spiritual connection between the two of us, no sense of being a 'soul mate'. And in my speaking and actions I sometimes asked, 'Is that me? Am I inadequate?' I feel frustrated by my partner's unwillingness to take emotional risks.

Cycles, Seasons and Tides

I hope I am in the latter part of winter, just before the spring and summer yet to come. Outside conditions can be bleak but within the earth the buds are getting ready to germinate and grow. Within apparent stillness much change is taking place and when conditions are right a new growth will rise up and bloom.

Intimacy and Commitment

To me, to be intimate means to be able to speak and listen, to not be judged, to be accepted as is, to know there are good bits and bad bits, to be willing to play with and explore both of these aspects, to be on a voyage of self-discovery and discovery of my partner, together, and to not have to hide or disguise aspects of myself.

Looking Back

My earlier adult life began with a sense of relief with my divorce from my first wife. It was not until years later that I was able to acknowledge to myself that I had married because of my own insecurity and fears that I would not be attractive to anyone else. I started with enthusiasm, selling my business, doing a computer course for a year and seriously contemplating a change of career. I fantasized about a life of working in various parts of the world needing only the skills and knowledge in my head.

Some seminars in Transactional Analysis made me aware that there was more to my behavior than I had realized and a brief passionate affair gave me a glimpse of how others viewed and lived their lives. Yet, I was still bound by my conditioning and the expectations that I had unthinkingly accepted from others.

I considered my situation rationally rather than emotionally and after deciding to return to my original profession I bought a business. During my year being a student again I had met a lady who was to become my second wife. She came to work in my business and the future looked bright. We had a purpose and we prospered. My professional skills advanced at a rapid rate and her skills managed the practice brilliantly.

We married but our hopes and aspirations floundered on our inability to even recognize, let alone deal with, our individual demons. We separated a few years later and it was during this stage that I started to appreciate the extent to which I was disassociated from my own feelings. I realized I was living only an outline of a life and that I had no idea of who I was, what I felt or what I even really wanted. I was internally driven to achieve, to be the best, to be successful and even while achieving these things I never felt comfort or pleasure in them.

A sense of unease and imminent disaster was with me all the time. I lived a life but rarely enjoyed it. My wife and I reconciled, bought a house and started again. This period was exhilarating as well as painful as I struggled to be honest with myself and to learn to recognize and accept not only my inadequacies but also those of my wife and all the other people that passed through my life. During this time there were several occasions where I nearly left the relationship, but each time I stayed, agonizing whether I had stayed through fear of the unknown or whether I was getting better at dealing with conflict and anger rather than withdrawing as my father had done, permanently, when I was only five years old.

My involvement with ***The Men's Group*** *as well as various personal-growth programs led to a calmer emotional space. The death of my grandmother, my father-in-law and a close friend during those years made me aware of my own mortality and I developed a slightly easier view of the world.*

My sense of imminent disaster eased and I became more comfortable with the idea of being able to let go of things and to live a simpler life. I realized that my view of life was up to me, and that to a very large extent, I could choose to be happy or not. I could choose to feel satisfied or not.

The other very exciting thing was to accept that the reactions others stirred in me were an important lesson about who I was, more than about who they were. I came back to that lesson time and time again. I needed to learn this and it was then that, for the first time, I could seriously contemplate a more reflective life. One in which I could go back to music, photography, maybe even do a course in literature or writing, mediate a little, enjoy fine wines and perhaps even accept the idea that, just maybe, enough could be enough.

Fathers

My parents separated when I was 5 years old and I saw my father three times after that. The first time was when he had me for the weekend shortly after the divorce (of which I have no recollection). The second time when he came to the primary school when I was about 7 or 8 years old and spent an hour or so, promising a bicycle that never came and the third time when my mother and I buried him when I was about 19 or 20.

What I learned from my father was withdrawal. What I didn't get from him were the things that fathers and sons are meant to do together. I learnt to be self-sufficient and self-contained. Ultimately I can only rely on myself. People make promises that they may or may not keep. It is unwise to feel joy on the expectation; wait for the reality. Another thing I didn't get was some acknowledgment that I was alive, that he felt some connection and that he cared about me. He never saw his daughter, my sister – not even one time. How can a man father two children and just stay away?

Is my sense of responsibility so strong in reaction to his irresponsibility? Am I scared to appear irresponsible even though being responsible may be harming me? There is a void in my life. Would I have been a good father? What would it have been like to be a father's son?

The Movement of Men

I found my way to this men's group as part of trying to understand my self and what was happening in my life. My expectations were negative and defensive at first and gradually changed to openness and a feeling of safety and acceptance. It became so as I listened to the other men speak and heard my life echoed in their words. Gradually I developed the courage to speak of my experiences and feelings and found that the sharing with the others helped to change me. The acceptance of other men of me and of themselves helped me to go beyond my defenses and taught me that I could be open and honest and that by doing so I became stronger, not weaker. I learned that we make our own realities. I learned that what we see in others is a reflection of what we feel within ourselves and that others can be our most effective teachers even during the most unpleasant confrontations.

My journey has been uncomfortable, exhilarating, sad and happy. It will never be complete but I like its direction.

My Eulogy

Scott was always curious.

There was nothing that he wouldn't be interested in.

He expressed this in his professional life by going far beyond his basic training and achieving standards matched by very few.

In his personal growth he was always open to seeing things in a new way and was always keen to learn more about himself.

He was willing to take risks emotionally and professionally, and to stand up for what he believed to be true, though it went against the prevailing orthodoxy.

Scott mellowed in his later years but still retained a playfulness that could wind people up. He became more accepting of others' weaknesses as he became more accepting of his own.

Scott's ability to immerse himself in things that interested him was quite remarkable; there were never half measures and he never quit until he felt he had mastered the subject. It was often only then that he could enjoy it for himself rather than for the challenge it posed.

For all his growth over the years, there was always a part in Scott that strived to prove itself over and over. This intensity could be off-putting to some.

In his life, however, Scott always had a kind spirit and would never knowingly cause deliberate pain.

He was slow to anger and quick to laugh.

Those who took the trouble to get close reaped the reward of his caring, non-judging warmth and loyalty.

We will remember you!

Tim

Relationships

Rejection, for me was not just a word, but also an act that so powerfully drove me into fear. When my father died, I was seven years old and my mother was so distressed and angry with him leaving that the six children were never allowed or encouraged to talk about Dad. There were no photos in the home and for me the loss was devastating. Of course, I didn't realize this then.

So, from seven, I can now see why suddenly this confident little boy became so scared. Mother would drag me to school and I would develop many tricks to get back home. This rejection of my mother towards her husband was now transferred to me. Not only had I lost my dad, but also I was not given the opportunity to say goodbye and complete with him leaving. Of course, I didn't know that and my mother obviously did not as she wouldn't have consciously inflicted this onto the children she obviously loved. That is why she was so angry; angry that he left her with six children to raise on her own.

My life as a boy was always a mixture of seeking attention, getting into trouble, and then the fear. This fear I was ashamed of because deep down I knew I was a coward. Why couldn't I feel strong as a soldier? Why did every topic involving rejection bring up so much fear?

Of course this didn't get any better as I quickly found a girl relationship. She became my wife. My wife had also been rejected as a child as her father had left her too. It is interesting how we were attracted to each other.

These days I now come closer to dealing with my fears. Having learnt a little, I feel more confident and stronger, and I can now feel happier about my father.

Cycles, Seasons and Tides

I am in summer presently within a rich harvest. The abundance of material things has allowed my partner and me to spend more time together in a relaxed and accepting way. We have worked hard together to bring about this season. All around me feels good now with most areas of my life making sense and having a clarity that I have not often seen. It's as if I am watching what happens around me as a true observer with a new found ability to choose what I will get into, what feelings I will take on, and without a need to force my beliefs or judgments on others. This is a beautiful calm form of freedom, temporarily.

The world around me is like a dangerous jungle with many people representing dangerous things that can happen to me. I am now hoping that through what I have learnt and the acceptance of myself as a mere man, no better, no worse, no different to anyone else that I may have the strength within to tackle the certain challenges that are coming. I know summer will not last and this realization is in itself a great gift to me as future seasons can come and go with me accepting them and feeling confident I will remain OK.

Intimacy and Commitment

I feel wrongly judged when it comes to intimacy. As a man I have feelings and of course sexual drive, and for me having had no previous experience in intimacy made being good at this quite difficult. I do not like having 'just sex' and there are times when I am satisfied to just be together. My experience, however, is that our relationship was tarnished because my wife was rejected by her father, and I was rejected by my father. Our relationship has finally come to terms with this rejection and I feel like I have been found innocent after a long trial. Intimacy is now truly starting for me.

Looking Back

Life was mostly great at the time I was writing this. There was an abundance of work and opportunity for me and I found it easy to succeed because I loved to work hard. People were rewarded for working hard and you could earn good money and buy many things like houses and cars and holidays!

For me, it was also a great time of learning as I grew with my young children and tried to learn more of life and what it all meant. Excitement reigned supreme in my early adulthood as I grew in my job, traveled to other parts of the Australia and the world. We had some great holidays as a family, also, and I even took my son on a camping adventure to Ayers Rock and we camped under the stars and wondered at the beauty. We also worried about being attacked by Aborigines. It was great to be so free, and chose most of what we did.

Of course, life was not always just fun and there were many problems too. I feared being hated as I was sacking people and I didn't like playing God. I had problems in my marriage that took great patience and pain before it was understood. Once I understood it, it was pretty easy to fix. So I have had a great time as I grew stronger as a provider, and, I think, as a person, too. It was a period of fabulous learning.

Life for me has been wonderful. I say wonderful because I have been given the opportunity to see all the wonders of life, both the good and the bad. My journey through life had great times of fun.

As a boy searching for tadpoles, building billy carts, playing sport and playing with firecrackers. These times were fabulous with a feeling of freedom and excitement.

However, there were times in between the excitement that I missed my father so much that it really hurt. I think he loved me so much that when he died (I was only seven) it made it even worse. No one spoke of him and there were no photos. Looking back, I became very scared.

Life went on and the excitement continued, and in between my years I had moments of real confidence and power, moments of great insight and a feeling that I must succeed. My life became more successful and I felt great pride as I became stronger and more independent. Today, I still fear rejection, still strive to be loved and as I learn more of life itself, I become somewhat stronger and more respectful of the difficulties of just growing up as a man. We men have many responsibilities and many battles to win. You will have some difficulties too. So be careful to care for yourself, on your journey as I hope your life is as rich for you as mine was for me.

Fathers

My father died when I was seven but I did learn some things from him. Mostly, I remember him giving me a small toy when I was sick. He was so good to me.

My dad was a soldier and one day I asked him to bring home a jeep. That weekend he brought home a jeep and we took some of my mates for a drive. Of course, everyone else in the family, my three sisters, especially, said I was spoilt rotten and always got what I wanted.

One day, I hid on the back floor of the car and didn't say 'boo', until we arrived at camp. My dad just took me into camp for the day and taught me how to play darts with the other soldiers.

So he taught me heaps because he showed real love to me as a child. I suppose this would have changed as I grew older but I will never know since he just died and I never saw him again.

He also taught me that I should love my children like he loved me, but sometimes I don't know how to love my son since he is 19 years old and I just don't know. I wish my dad had stayed with me longer than he did.

Work

Work for me is a place where I can express my organizational abilities with people. I have the opportunity to help others to develop and it's like a journey where we pick up new challenges, make changes and work with everyone to make it happen! Work is demanding, rewarding and good fun a lot of the time.

Work can bring about many emotions. In a time of change I can feel overloaded and weighed down. However, the desire to conquer and win drives me to find a way to succeed. It can keep the bullshit in perspective. Work is fine.

What I get from work is a lot of satisfaction and personal reward from my work. I feel this is what I am good at and enjoy contributing to the team. I feel valued by the team and believe I help others in many ways.

The Movement of Men

My involvement with **The Men's Group** *started shortly after my wife had what is commonly referred to as a 'nervous breakdown'. I now realize that people carry many issues around like excess baggage that eventually weighs them down to the point of not coping.*

I was recommended to join the men's group and went initially with a view of keen interest to understand and learn how to help my wife. To my surprise, I found myself entering a new dimension of learning, a perspective that gave me better coping skills, more confidence that I was okay and worthy and a feeling that I could actually help.

The men's group initially opened my eyes to many new ways of viewing people and a better understanding of how relationships work. There have been many experiences during the meetings that have brought great insight into my life. This has given me more strength and skills in relating to my family, children and my wife.

My life these days is more balanced. I see things much more clearly, and I feel less stress and guilty. I know now that many of the worries and issues I have are normal for us 'men' and accepting the fact that I am an okay person has been a great confidence booster for me. I have learnt to deal with many of my fears and while I still remain challenged continually by the men's group, I hope I can keep connected to this great forum of men in the years to come and continue the inspiration.

My Eulogy

Tim was a man that could always be relied on and to many people that knew him well would appreciate how honest and dedicated he was to everyone around him.

Tim was a keen family man and while he and his wife were married at a young age he always tried his hardest to be a good husband and provider.

Tim loved helping people and was always keen to listen to others without judgment but with a keen desire to really listen and understand.

His guidance and understanding of life generally often helped put things back into balance.

One of the great gifts a man can have is one of integrity and honor. Tim was a man that had both of these qualities, and expected others to have them also but as he grew older became more and more forgiving of the faults of others.

While we will all miss Tim we can also reflect on the cheerful character and the happiness that he brought to so many people. Tim will always want us to remember him as a true friend on an adventure to be closer to the truth and with love.

Umar

Relationships

Criticism and rejection are things I became familiar with very early in my life (my conception was an 'accident'). Hence I never felt truly bonded to or felt loved by my mother and the reverse is also true. Rejection is hard to deal with in relationships because, in my opinion, a relationship is a way of communion of feelings, ideals, means and ways of realizing my and my partner's future. We see part of us in the other and we let part of this other in us, so that when I am rejected I am first of all hurt in the deepest parts of my Self.

Criticism also hurts a hell of lot because it means that I don't measure up to my partner's expectations that result in anger and fear of rejection. The negative reactions ultimately point to the fact that I may have to take a look at myself and put in a lot of painful work and change what I am (a very scary thing for me).

Cycles, Seasons and Tides

At this moment in my life I feel I am in the spring of my Self. The external things like study, kids, material wealth, etc. are as good as they get. The internal ones, my relationship with myself and my wife are ever changing, ever developing, whereby I feel different about them every day like on an endless journey where the traveling is more important than the destination.

I am sounding the depth of my Self and discovering new ways of experiencing the warmth of inner love for my Self and my partner. I am laying the groundwork for an even better appreciation of life and my place in the universe. The summer will take care of itself as will autumn and winter. I am just discovering how to let go and go with the flow.

Intimacy and Commitment

Personally I think women are better or more adept to talk about or be intimate because they have been practicing it from the start. As babies, women are cuddled and spoken to softly, gently, whereas males are picked up, held up and told how they are going to be tall, strong, etc.

Females are always with their mums or other women with whom they have a loving relationship and they are trained to discuss (bitch) about other people's affairs (usually intimate, personal ones). It's different for boys; they are given toy guns and sent away to play cowboys and Indians, cops and robbers, and Dad doesn't get very intimate as he only discusses footy, wrestles with his son etc.

Hence, when it comes to intimacy, females and males speak a different language. For females, intimacy means love and caring. For males (me) intimacy means weakness, which is not the right behavior.

Looking Back

Every man has got a story and here's mine. I would like to tell you how grateful and fortunate I have been. Whilst growing up I learnt many things I thought were the right ones to know: how to be a father, a husband, and a person! I learnt these from my parents and they in turn learnt them from their respective parents. But, although these were things I thought I needed to 'make it' in life, they didn't seem to solve 'my' problems.

I had a sense of emptiness, lack of purpose and other negative feelings flowing from these, until slowly I began to see these things as the wrong solutions to 'my' problems. I began to feel and be a totally different person, a different man. These changes necessitated a lot of pain and digging into my heart. But it was pain with a purpose.

The prize was too precious to ignore, even when the pain got to be unbearable, as I knew that everything worthwhile in life requires pain. Through these changes, I discovered the 'old' things I had learnt and leant 'new' ones: to be comfortable as me and to be gentle, yet masculine at the same time. I learnt to connect with the man within me that has remained unchanged throughout the thousands of years that man has been man. I understand this energy in me that I thought was simply aggressiveness. I understand why I sometimes feel that need for solitude. I now appreciated the difference between woman and man, and I learnt to trust your mother's qualities and insights as a woman.

Son, my life as a man is exciting beyond my wildest expectations, feeling in charge, yet not attached to life, being open and receptive to all possibilities fate offers. You will also grow and I will be there to help you and show you how to bring out from within you the same energy that makes adults into men. So that you may experience the same balance and love I feel for my Self and those around me.

Fathers

In spite of all the pain I suffered growing up in my family, I learned that my dad valued honesty (at least as it is seen by the man in the street). That is why, perhaps, I seem to be preoccupied about always doing the 'right thing'.

I also learned, in moments of sincere and open discussion, that my father once was himself a child; he wasn't 'always' my father. He also told me how he had an abysmal relationship with his father and mother, and that he didn't want the same for me. I learned that, although he could not see it, he had indeed repeated his history (kicking the shit out of his kids and his wife, etc.). Things that my dad taught me are that seeing the sort of father, husband, man he was, and the unhappiness in his life, perhaps I should find new different solutions to my life and not follow his path (although it has been very hard to do otherwise).

What I didn't receive from my father was simply being there for me, to check how my life was going, to do things together. I would have loved to be accepted without judgment, to be loved with affection; whereas he was simply the man who was never home because he had to provide for the family.

The Movement of Men

In my case, the reason for joining men's groups is primarily to find who the 'real' Umar is, as opposed to Umar the husband, Umar the son, Umar the brother, etc.

It is also a way and means to outgrow my limitations imposed on me by those around me as I was growing as a child and a young man; limitations that I eagerly took on board to the extent that I thought were traits of my personality and from which I derived my identity.

***The Men's Group** is also a way for me to see other men in a different light, to see the softness in them, feelings, in other words. I, like many others, usually only see the 'hard' side of man. Personally, I still find it difficult to interact with men in a position of authority. This is something that stems from my relationship with my father.*

***The Men's Group** offers me a chance and means to connect with other men and to feel comfortable with them on a level much deeper than I ever could otherwise in my 'everyday' environment.*

My Eulogy

Umar was a man who like many others, came into being not out of love and in love, but simply due to an 'accident'. That fact had a major impact on his life and colored his perception of who he was and how others viewed him.

He walked around carrying deep wounds and most of all, always eager to play the part that he thought was his to play in life: the selfless helper to others (mother, father, brothers, sister), 'fixer' of his parents problems and marriage and the dumb student at school (because that's what his mother said he was).

He was always searching for love and approval (that he felt he didn't get from his parents) from others. That was who Umar was for many years, despite 'growing up' into a 'man'.

Then a chance to grow came along and to his credit he seized it with both hands (and all his heart), and learnt that, to a large extent, he had been playing someone else's part thinking someone else's thoughts, going through someone else's pain.

With lots of heartache, honesty and truth, he learnt that he didn't have to be what he thought he had to be.

He could be everything he thought he couldn't (or shouldn't) be! (It was even okay to fuck-up and still be positive about it!)

Umar subsequently went on to blossom into a wonderful, loving, affectionate, peaceful man! Things just got better and better! He married a sweet girl who was ready and willing to embark on a process of growth that led them to feel emotions that they thought didn't exist, as they had not experienced these emotions (such as intimacy, tranquility or trust) in their respective families.

Umar went on to have a child with his companion and felt good and serene about it because he knew he had given his son the biggest gift of all: he had broken the chain. He would be able to give unconditional love.

Umar died after having achieved in life more than he ever could dream. The man who died was not the same person that was born years ago, because he had realized that change is the most important thing in life and he knew he would be ready to continue his journey in the next life.

Victor

Relationships

Rejection is the hardest thing for me in relationships. Rejection brings to the fore feelings of abandonment, unworthiness and helplessness that I first experienced as a child in response to parental rejection and that were reinforced by peer rejection in adolescence.

To be denied love, warmth and affection, to be rejected because of who I am, and to know there is nothing I can do to gain the love and regard I crave is the hardest way to learn the mystery that I am alone and at the same time part of a greater whole.

Being rejected by the ones I would love has taught me to face myself and to accept my Self, as I am, a unique part of the universe. It has taught me that love does not originate in the loved one, or within myself, but that love's origin is the source of life itself and that love flows from that source and through me into the world. I can only allow that love to flow through me to another, and gladly receive love that flows back to me, regardless of where it comes from.

Cycles, Seasons and Tides

I have emerged from the long winter of the soul, the 'mid-life crisis', into early spring. Winter began about ten years ago with bouts of depression, binge drinking, womanizing and unfocussed rage, darkened into deepest despair in which everything in my life was meaningless and alien, and then shifted through a chance encounter with Peter O'Connor's book, 'Understanding the Mid-Life Crisis'. I then realized that what I was alienated from was my feminine nature, my soul.

I had constructed an external life, which shut out so much of myself the hard-edged work in social statistics, my wife on whom I had laid the burden of my feminine side, the aloof, cynical shell I had developed for protection, the dreams and artistic talent I had abandoned ('not good enough', 'can't make a living out of that'). I realized that I had become a stranger to myself.

Then the really hard work began learning how I had brought this about, developing a new way of being, relapsing into despair, surviving the disintegration of my old external life and the aloof shell. As the changes within me gathered strength, as the winter ice began to thaw and the river of life began to flow more and more strongly my external life changed when and as it had to.

My marriage went first, as I fell into another relationship so powerful and passionate that it swept me into the whirlpool of projecting my soul onto my lover. Fortunately that relationship also faltered and I was left face-to-face, at last, with my Self and my greatest fear of being rejected and abandoned.

Here, in the longest, darkest night of winter, I came through the pain and fear to a reborn self: raw, vulnerable, tentative, uncertain of its power, but more truly me. From that beginning, I have emerged into early spring, developing a beautiful, mature relationship of great openness, commitment and love, changing my work from the job of social statistics to my vocation as a sculptor and healer, and dissolving the shell to live more openly from the heart, with passion and playfulness.

I feel like a newly born animal in the spring endlessly curious about life, seriously playful, making mistakes and learning from them, sometimes tentative, sometimes bold, but always feeling the power of aliveness surging through me.

Intimacy and Commitment

I was terrified of intimacy and commitment in my first marriage. I followed my childhood pattern of always holding back my innermost self. Commitment was qualified. Intimacy was hedged about and limited. I was secretive, always keeping my deepest feelings and thoughts buried so deeply sometimes that even I wasn't aware of them.

Not prepared to commit to myself, I could not and would not commit to a relationship. I lived a double life. On the surface, the good husband and father, an honest and kind person. In private, the seducer of women, the boozer, the trickster, the ruthless, amoral playboy, the addict.

Only by coming through the pain and fear of rejection and abandonment and by being forced to be alone before the Higher Power, could I learn to commit to myself, above all else to being true to my inner self.

Only by committing to myself and being intimate with my true feelings could I learn how to commit to a relationship and accept the intimacy of simply being open hearted with another open heart. Only by committing to me, could I commit to an 'us'.

Looking Back

Dear Grandson,

You have asked me what life was like for me as a young man. It was a time when great social changes deepened and consolidated. It was a time when I began to discover the dynamic balance and wholeness of what I had believed until then were irreconcilable opposites.

I came to value the complementarities of logic, intellect, hard-edged masculinity and science. I became more aware of the value of insight, intuition, the feminine values of feeling and caring and spirituality. The most exciting revelations, for part of me, occurred in the field of science with the discovery of order emerging from chaos – the realization that the universe is fundamentally a dance of patterned energy emerging from a void of potentiality and that, once manifested in matter, this universal energy displays the characteristics of purposeful intelligence. This confirmed what I had learned through studying ancient philosophies such as Taoism: that there is a single source of energy infinitely manifested. For me, the most exciting discovery was that I could experience this energy directly.

By facing my fears, moving through the pain of change, clearing my mind and opening my heart, I allowed my intuition and feeling to guide me to the Divine energy within myself and of all things. I felt a love, a joy and a sense of aliveness I had never known before. I learned to work with, rather than against, the natural flow of energy in all areas of my life; in fathering my children, in encouraging the earth to bring forth food and flowers, in expressing my wisdom through my work.

Indeed, work has become for me no longer a job, a chore to be endured, but a means for expressing my masculine energy. It became play to be enjoyed, a vocation to channel the universal energy in loving service to benefit others and an art form to fulfill my innermost self. I became more truly a man strong with love, powerful in spirit as well as in deeds, capable of bringing my dreams into being.

Fathers

The things that I most remember learning from my father are those that I am painfully and slowly unlearning now: avoidance of the difficult, survival through concealment, suppression of feelings, wariness of authority and fear of power. He was of the generation for whom manliness meant physical strength, stoic endurance of physical pain, protection of women and children, career and monetary success.

During my childhood, my father was well on his way to becoming an alcoholic. Strength became violence, protection of his wife and child became domination, and his work eroded his life and ours. He rejected me time and again because I wasn't physically strong or skilled at sports, feared physical pain, I was a sensitive, feeling, imaginative child. I lived in fear that he would lose control, that the smacking would become a bashing. I lived in fear that the sexual abuse would be repeated. I lived in fear that he would kill my mother and me in a fit of alcoholic rage. I withered under his insults and sarcasm. I learned to keep out of his way, to conceal my true feelings, to live my own life in secret.

Looking back, I realize, with some awe, how brave and indomitable my spirit was as a child. What I wanted most from my father was acceptance, acceptance of me simply as I was.

The Movement of Men

The men's sharing I have experienced has taught me that my story is not unique. So many men have experienced damaged lives as children and adolescents. So many men have lacked the teaching of older men and the access that it can provide to the protective and pragmatic power and wisdom of maleness. So many men have failed to be wise and nurturing partners and fathers.

The men's sharing has also given me faith in the power of the group to foster healing. We can, through sharing our pain, our fears, our joys and our passions, purify our maleness. We can re-connect with the source of pure male energy, a non-manipulative power that alters the physical world that protects, nurtures and fosters growth towards its natural fulfillment that brings our dreams into reality.

We can also re-connect with the feminine energy of the intuitive, imaginative, creative, feeling power that provides vision and inner wisdom. We can become more truly men, strong, enduring, wise and nurturing practical dreamers.

My Eulogy

We are gathered here today to say our final farewell to Victor who has died and merged with the light of which he so often spoke.

It is easy to dwell on his achievements, particularly those of the latter half of his life when he contributed so much through his art, his writing and his healing work. But these were only the trace of the man, the mark of his spirit as it moved through this life.

His greatest creation was his own life and the way his spirit touched and uplifted ours.

Deeply committed to his wife and children, he gave selflessly of himself to uplift and encourage their growth, and he received as much love and wisdom from them as he gave.

What we will miss most about Victor are the deeper things that moved through him: his warmth, love and understanding; his active and practical compassion for others; the way he uplifted and inspired those whose lives he touched directly or through his art and writing; his passion about life; his larger-than-life love of life; the exultation and joy that poured through him; his wisdom and insight that he shared so openly with others; his courage in facing the truth about himself; and his living true to his inner, higher Self.

Victor, we bid you a swift passage to the home of your spirit.

Holding your memory in our hearts, we thank you for so enriching our lives.

Walter

Relationships

I've always had a deep fear of rejection. This seems to manifest itself in many ways that tend to have an adverse effect on my authenticity. The prime example is the way I avoid upsetting anyone close to me. That means I keep criticisms to myself. I don't talk about things that upset or disappoint me and I try to fulfill other people's expectations, or at least my perception of what their expectations might be!

I find that I have turned into, or trained myself to be something of a social chameleon. I can change my color to suit the mood and what's going on around me with such ease that I am not even aware of it most of the time. I feel that in doing this, I am stripping my Self of any personality or spirit of my own, turning myself into some kind of soulless pleaser.

Another example is how I always try very hard to look good, attractive, strong, clever, athletic, funny, happy, thoughtful, etc., etc. How I look to someone else is never far from my consciousness. I suppose my strategy in this is that if others see things in me that they want, and then they will want me to be part of their life. The catch is that sometimes I get so good at looking good that it alienates those whom I am trying to impress. I look so good that they think I couldn't possibly want to have anything to do with them. And I am concentrating so hard on my task that even if someone does try to make a connection to me, I cannot respond authentically and I lose it!

Cycles, Seasons and Tides

I feel I am on the cusp of two seasons at the moment. I am still in the season of awakening and learning about a life of openness and the possibilities that come with that. But at the same time, I feel I am moving into a season of putting into practice these things I have been learning.

It feels a bit like the transition from spring to summer. Winter seems long in the past, but not forgotten. Spring has been a time of awakening and growth, nourishment. I have awakened to a whole different way of being, of openness and authenticity.

I have begun to grow, receiving the nourishment of the advice, encouragement, nurturing shared experiences and acceptance of some wonderful people around me. The springtime, which I don't think is quite over yet, is allowing me to grow so strongly and quickly that I can feel the summer. It is so very close now. I can envisage myself playing on that wonderful, endless beach of life, under that warm sun of love and openness. I am surrounded by a wonderful crowd of people, all of us immersed in the sheer joy and love of life and freedom. That sounds like a really nice season and the anticipation is... oh... so sweet.

Intimacy and Commitment

Fear of intimacy and/or commitment in a relationship with a woman has never been an issue for me. In fact, intimacy and commitment are things I desperately search for in a new relationship. Hmm... now that I think about it... my experience of a no-longer-new relationship (I have been with my partner for 15 years) hints to me that maybe there are some issues there for me.

I have noticed that when I look at a woman I do more than simply enjoy her beauty. Almost always I find myself assessing her as a potential partner. Measuring her up. Why? Well, I never know when I might be in the market for a new partner. Does anyone? How on earth can I be truly committed to my life's partner when there is stuff like than inside me every day?

Not only am I assessing women, of course, I am also searching for signs that they might be similarly assessing me. This is how I check my own 'marketability'. Do I still have a chance on the singles scene?

Am I a sick puppy? No. I think I am probably pretty normal in this regard. But I do feel a bit frustrated that I don't feel completely content with what I have in life and that I am constantly on the lookout for 'more' or 'better'.

Also, it's pretty hard to be honest and almost impossible to be upfront about these feelings, especially with my partner. I wonder if I should let her read this!

Looking Back

The early years as an adult were very exciting times with amazing advances in technology and constant shifts in business focus areas. There were dynamic years, full of possibilities, but at the same time so very competitive and even cutthroat.

I found the times to be quite scary, even though I had a good, reliable employer and a good career with excellent salary and conditions. I guess I felt I had so much to lose if anything went wrong. It was a bit of a roller coaster ride, really, easy to get on, thrilling and frightening to ride, and a feeling that I had no control at all!

When I think of those days, most of my thoughts seem to revolve around work and career and making the right investments, planning for the future. It's no wonder the governments of the day had so little direction, vision, or substance. They were primarily driven by economic considerations. We get what we deserve. Fortunately, the great crash of the late-eighties was a cloud with a silver lining. Many people began to see the mad speculation for what it was, and they began to take stock, realizing that money was merely a means to an end.

This feeling developed and grew and more people found themselves searching for something more in life than the never-ending climbing, earning and spending cycle. From this emerged that wonderful era around the turn of the century when people began actually relating to one another again and relationships developed along with people's sense of self.

You may find it amazing now, but back in the latter part of last century, strangers did not speak to each other on trains! In fact, they didn't even look at each other for fear of being spoken to! Thank goodness, those days are long gone, but we need to remember that that was the beginning of the wonderful, dynamic melting pot of humanity we see today, with beautiful, confident people relating to one another on a truly deep and personal level, able to be completely sincere and completely authentic in every way. The concept of competition fostering an unhealthy atmosphere now seems impossible, and I count myself lucky.

Fathers

From my father learnt to be silent and to not talk about my feelings. I learnt that certain things are just too hard to talk about or deal with.

I learnt to go about my work in a quiet and industrious way, not drawing undue attention to myself.

I learnt a logical way of thinking and ways of reasoning things out.

I learnt a quiet, gentle and warm sense of humor.

I learnt a fascination for tools and a love of building things. Unfortunately, though, I wasn't able to serve any kind of apprenticeship under him to learn to make things. I could observe but was not allowed to get involved in the projects and help. I would only watch and mostly couldn't even ask questions and expect a reasonable answer. I would have loved to be able to do things with him, but he wanted to do them on his own.

The Movement of Men

A relationship breakdown brought me to seek out counseling and here I found myself invited to join ***The Men's Group****. I joined the group initially because the breakdown of my relationship had allowed me to feel that something was missing in my life. In fact, I was feeling like a great many things were missing.*

I was in search of these missing pieces. I needed to know what they were to start with! I saw the men's group as a possible tool to help me get my head together. What I found was a community, a wonderful, strong, searching and nurturing community that is free of competition and judgment.

At first, it was very confronting. I had a lot of shame inside me and I didn't want to talk about it. Everyone else seemed to be so honest and forthright and I was holding back.

After awhile, I learnt some acceptable kinds of things to say and was more comfortable, but still not very honest.

After awhile longer, as I felt more and more comfortable, I started to be able to speak from the heart. When this first began to be possible I was completely overwhelmed by the energy I brought to the group. In seeing what a powerful experience it had been for other members of the group when I finally opened up, I could finally feel good about not hiding my feelings. This has been an incredibly freeing experience. The more I practice openness in such a nurturing environment, the more it comes naturally to me.

Then there is the other side of the coin. To be present when another man pours out his innermost feelings without reserve, sometimes with great anger and often sadness, is a beautiful experience of trust. It is also quite amazing to see how many of our fears and frustrations are common to so many other men. These are the things that block us from really living life and it is wonderful to be able to share experiences of these hurtful things and gain strength from the group. We no longer have to shoulder the burden on our own!

Eulogy

Walter was a man who loved other people; always finding ways to help where there was a need and to give comfort where there was pain.

He was always striving to find ways to share what wisdom he had found himself and show others that life is to be lived and enjoyed.

He did this by leading by example, allowing and encouraging anyone who saw the possibilities to join him.

While setting and achieving goals was important to him, he always managed to inject some fun into his work, managing to strike a rare and beautiful balance in life.

To be with Walter often meant making challenges to be accepted and safe ways of doing things, which made his life and lives of those around him a constant adventure.

He would not allow himself to be held back by senseless rules or conventions, but did not ignore or devalue the feelings of others.

Walter was a sensitive and open man, unafraid to allow his feelings, to be seen.

He was a living example of how beautiful, challenging, satisfying and joyous life can be.

Those of us fortunate enough to have been touched by his life will forever count our blessings and in difficult times will be able to think of him and remember not to surrender hope.

Walter showed us that a wondrous and authentic life is not only a possibility, but that we should settle for nothing less.

Xavier

Relationships

Criticism, rejection, disrespect, being taken for granted for me, it's summed up in one word: dishonor. I think that is what I find hardest to deal with – being dishonored within a family, or a relationship. This comes from a deep conviction within me that I will never be with a woman who dishonors me.

I don't think this is coming from the ego. I am happy to accept the machinations of a relationship. I know it is one of the most difficult and complex tasks life offers me.

For me, dishonor means a disregard for the Spirit. It is a refusal by a partner to accept that there could be more to me than meets the eye, that I am something more than this body, this breadwinner, this responsible family man, this oh so nice guy. I don't think it is a benign quality. Dishonor seems to have an attack to it, a constant picking away at the Spirit. It occurs over many years. I don't think it comes from the ego, rather through the ego.

A partner who is unaware of, or denies the Spirit, sets about belittling the other at the deepest level, with words and actions that become almost habitual. It seems to me dishonoring causes a Spiritual pain. Can the Spirit really be hurt? Yes, or maybe eternal, unchanging, all pervading, a dewdrop in the pearly sea, but it can also weep like a child.

Cycles, Seasons and Tides

I see my life as a cycle, as the soil or land that provides the medium for the cycle of the crop. The soil is prepared, made ready, cared for.

The seeds are planted in the fresh, moist-rich soil. The young crops are watched, left to nature, open to the sun, to tempest, to danger. In time, it matures in a way that nature allows: then the harvest, the gathering and the rewards.

Now the soil lies fallow. It is resting. All the work is being done below the surface. The activity of the cycle is finished. The land appears ugly, just soil doing nothing. It has served its purpose, it has been cut up, used, made demands of, produced the goods and now it appears past its prime.

But this fallow land is rich in activity. Worms are busy, digging, turning, and opening the soil to the rain and sun and wind. This land is busy being this land and nothing else. This land exists as the essence of itself. It is not for anything now.

The soil is being renewed, being reshaped, re-vitalized, and made ready. The miracle of this resurrection is that it occurs with the solid just being itself, being worthy of a new cycle. By being true to itself it is now ready for a new crop.

So now I lie fallow. But beneath the surface the wonderful worms of the soul, with great love and tenderness, prepare me for a new seeding.

Intimacy and Commitment

I want a relationship as much as I don't want a relationship. A deeply committed relationship entrances me, but also terrifies me. How do I accommodate this paradox in my life? Where does it come from?

I once saw a film of day's game of cricket taken from the air. The film of a day's play was condensed into a few minutes. As the fieldsmen changed positions the movement made the game like a breathing, living entity. I wonder if a good relationship would look the same way: the coming together, and moving apart being the pulse of a living thing, the vital force of the relationship, coming from the distance apart as much as from the closeness of the partners.

For me, it takes as much courage to be uncommitted and distant as it does to be close. It takes a fine relationship to allow each partner to be as they wish to be at that time, even if it means being distant. It comes back to a sense of self of each of the partners.

I wonder if it could be a matter of surrender. Surrender is something I find difficult. It suggests loss of control. Intimacy is surrender to that bewildering, terrifying feminine power. Commitment is surrender to a higher power. In the act of surrendering to a higher power could we overcome our fear of intimacy and commitment?

Looking Back

Oh, they were terrific years! In the last decade of the second millennium I went from 45 to 55. Those were major years in my life, but the experience of these years was heightened by the movement of energy in the hearts of both men and women.

The energy seemed to me to be a desire to 'come out'. It won't mean much to you now, but then to be gay was something to be hidden. Eventually, a man or a woman with enough courage would 'come out' and proclaim their sexuality to the world. I think with us at that time we were 'coming out' by proclaiming our spirituality to the world. I had seen the beginning of this energy in the writings of my mother. Her urge to express the feeling of a higher power, the presence of a higher power, was strong. But it was risky. Society was hard on such people.

But for us, it was an explosion of expression. Every conceivable way of expressing that spirit was undertaken. To me, a lot of it was rubbish, but even then it had an exciting mad energy about it. I was caught up in this 'rush' of spirituality. Millions were.

But the real work come later in the decade, when for many this settled down to a living or a manifestation of the Spirit in our everyday lives, which is where it was all the time, anyway. It was the gentle living of the Spirit that produced the major changes in life, the benefits you're now enjoying.

Fathers

I have a very early memory of standing with my father. We were both totally engrossed in what he was doing. I can still feel the wonderful union with him. It was the only time it happened. This is what I would have liked to receive: years of a gentle, unconscious union. I would have liked years of sharing his wisdom and experience. I would have liked his advice and guidance.

I learnt from him that being the opposite of him was an easier way of getting through life. He had left us, gone to gaol, was judged harshly. I became the good boy, was approved of, successful. I became the opposite of my father.

However, I met him later in life, and suddenly saw his beauty and his power. I saw his wildness, madness even. I saw him as a larrikin, with tremendous courage. I felt so proud that I was the son of this dark, wild, foolish man.

The Movement of Men

There were about twenty in the group... men who were all friends... men who had shared parts of their lives with each other. We were camping near Hepburn Springs and had gathered in an old open-cut gold mine. The moon was full and the ghostly light lit the contours of the land that had been brutalized in the search for gold. It was as if a giant claw had scooped up the land and turned it upside down and the deep parts of the earth brought to the surface. This land had been treated badly but with love and care was being healed.

In the group were Vietnam Veterans; there were men who had lived rough in the outback, men who had lived rough in Collins Street. All would welcome a physical challenge with gusto. But this weekend was to strike terror into our hearts. For this weekend we were to do NOTHING... no tasks, no appointments, no competitions, no rewards, no deadlines. We were to do NOTHING for three days.

I see Men's Movement as the movement of men's psyches, with men initiating in themselves changes in the way they see their world, and their behavior in that world. It is like the movement of energy through the psyches of men.

Like the line from Socrates, 'A life unexamined is a life unlived', this weekend in the wilderness forced us into self-examination and introspection. By stepping back from a normal life, even a normal weekend in the bush, we were able to see how much of our behavior was automatic. In that instant before acting we seemed to have no choice in the matter. It was time to examine the urge to compete and succeed constantly. Why could we in an instant lash out with words or fists with a ferocity that produced instant remorse? Why should a loving, kind, forgiving man turn into a raging beast because another driver impedes his progress through traffic lights?

Why indeed? We are touching very deep ground here. Where does this automatic behavior begin? Could it be in the non-anesthetized genital mutilation that many men suffered in the first days of their lives? I would imagine a baby would automatically shrink back from the next person who approached, after experiencing pain like that. But more likely, the cause is social conditioning, like the Jesuits say, 'Give me a boy until he is seven, and I'll have him for life'.

It's the scripts that are given to us during these years: 'Do your best'; 'You can do better than that'; 'You'll just have to try harder; 'Don't you ever let me see you cry again'; 'Quiet down, you're too excited'. This constant bombardment from significant elders is absorbed by the psyche and locked in forever. Scripts that drive us from the unconscious, until at thirty-five from the straight jacket of his conditioning a man cries, 'What am I doing? 'Is this all there is?' 'I am more than this.'

I have sat in many circles with many men, in rooms, in tents, on beaches, under the night sky. There is one movement that occurs every time. It is the nodding of heads. As a man hears his own story in another's words, his head nods not only in agreement, but also in amazement. 'I can't be hearing this... this life is the same as mine.' But it is true. Men's lives at their base have a deep and profound spiritual communion that goes back to the dawn of life. And this is the energy of the Men's Movement.

For in this communion lies validation. By telling our stories, by reliving the pain and sadness, by honoring the glory and triumphs, men can touch an anxiety spirit of strength and beauty. And they use this spirit for change.

Men have so much to give this planet. For so long this energy has been wasted on sharpness and violence, on mindless competition and control. It has been wasted on a dominating nature and brutalizing the earth. It is wasted at a subtle level on the inane battle of the sexes. It is so draining. It is killing men at a terrible rate.

Can you imagine this energy redirected to the good husbandry of the planet, towards the protection of its young with complete trust and safety? Imagine this energy directed to the honoring and respecting of the women of this earth, and the co-operation of the sexes in the enjoyment of this amazing gift that is life.

The Women's Movement was like a glorious skyrocket that burst on the planet with splendor and courage, releasing the built-up outrage of a hundred years. It was an explosion that changed our world forever.

The Men's Movement is more akin to the stirrings of a great bear as it begins to awake in its cave after the winter's hibernation. Its movements are slow and deliberate, but with a gentle grace. It stretches its arms and runs its mighty claws through the fur of its head, and with tremendous strength and ease it stands to its full height. Then, with an almost primal beauty and innocence he walks from the cave into the spring sunshine to begin life afresh.

My Eulogy

Xavier was a good friend to many.

He was loved by many.

He had both success and failure in his life.

He contributed to the planet, and took from the planet.

He really did have a deep, rich and complex life.

But for all this he was never quite happy with his life.

He often spoke of this 'bottomless pit of desire'.

He attempted to fill it with the love and approval of women: a wife, daughters... lover.

He tried to fill it with the love of friends.

He tried to fill it with the approval of his patients, his neighbors or his peers.

And, of course, all the love and approval in the world were forthcoming, but in those moments of aloneness the pit was absolutely bare.

All the love with universe could not put a tiny dent in this empty space.

I suppose you could say he was the classical existential fool, the angst of existence.

His greatest regret was that he took it all so seriously.

He looked so hard, missed so much lightness.

He was so intent on digging, on probing, on analyzing, on learning, that sometimes he felt that he had missed it all... missed all the light and laughter, and dwelt in the valley of the shadow of death.

His death must be familiar territory.

Acknowledgments

To my team of readers who were vigilant in not allowing this book to go ahead until they were totally satisfied that the message was presented in such a way that everyone would want to read it.

Thank you, my dear friends and fellow travelers Deborah Vaughan, Graeme Vaughan and Dr Peter Howe and Dr John Buckingham.

Thank you, my friend and fellow author, Veneta Tsindos.

Thank you, my publishing mentor and creative/technical director, Julie Postance, and editor and proofreader, Amanda Spedding.

Thank you to the foundation of my being my wife, Joy, and family who continue to love and support me, even when I am negligent in my receiving and giving of that love and support.

MenSpeak Author

Paul Mott is a psychotherapist in private practice in Melbourne, Australia. His vast and varied experience has been in education, business, government and counseling.

In the mid-80s, Paul left the corporate, academic and government worlds and began his private practice. Since going into private practice he has facilitated numerous groups since 1985 for men, women, individuals, couples, groups, organizations, and businesses. One such group was called *The Men's Group*, which ran for 15 years.

Paul was born and spent his childhood in Pennsylvania and early adulthood overseas and in California and Colorado. In the mid-70s, with his wife and three children he moved to Australia taking up academic positions at Australian universities including in Western Australia and then in Armadale, New South Wales, where he became a Senior Lecturer in curriculum design, language development and developmental psychology. He has also been a manager of private businesses, ran a hall of residence, served as Director of Pre-School Child Development and Director of Policy and Program Development with the Victorian Government in Australia. He was the first male kindergarten teacher in Colorado in the 1970s.

Paul has been married since 1968, has three adult children and five grandchildren.

He has previously written *Language Arts, A Source Book, Art Lessons for Students by Students, We're People* and *Reading Readiness.*

Work with Paul

Paul Mott is a psychotherapist in private practice in Melbourne, Australia. Paul Mott offers private counselling, group facilitation, workshops, online courses and retreats. Please contact Paul at paulmottauthor@gmail.com if you are interested in any of the following:

- Individual Counseling
- Couple's Counseling
- Men's Group Facilitation
- Couples Mediation
- Group Facilitation for Organizations and Businesses
- Men's One Day Workshop
- Men's Weekend
- Men's Online Seminar Series
- Men's One Week Retreat
- Couple's One Week Retreat
- Journey to Self One Week Retreat
- The Men's Finishing School

See Paul's website for more information: *www.menspeak.co*
Follow Paul on Twitter: *@PaulMottAuthor*
Like Paul on Facebook: *www.facebook.com/MenSpeak*
Email Paul directly at *paulmottauthor@gmail.com*

Coming Soon

Look out for Paul Mott's other books and courses!

The You That I Am Online Course
Paul Mott and Don Munro

Be
Paul and Joy Mott

Wisdom Within for Kids of All Ages
Joy Mott with Paul

A Primer for Couple Relationships
Paul and Joy Mott

The Kalgoorlie Kids
Joy Mott with Paul

PoArty (Poems with Art)
Paul Mott with Joy

www.ingramcontent.com/pod-product-compliance
Lightning Source LLC
LaVergne TN
LVHW091215080426
835509LV00009B/1000

* 9 7 8 0 9 9 4 1 8 1 6 0 2 *